Recruitment, Retention, and Restructuring: Human Resources in Academic Libraries

Ad Hoc Task Force on Recruitment & Retention Issues

a subcommittee of the
**Personnel Administrators and
Staff Development Officers
Discussion Group**

**Association of College and
Research Libraries**

Association of College and Research Libraries
A division of the American Library Association
Chicago 2002

The paper used in this publication meets the minimum requirements of American National Standard for Information Sciences–Permanence of Paper for Printed Library Materials, ANSI Z39.48—1992.∞

Library of Congress Cataloging-in-Publication Data
Association of College and Research Libraries. Ad Hoc Task
  Force on Recruitment & Retention Issues.
  Recruitment, retention & restructuring : human resources in
  academic libraries : a white paper / by the Ad Hoc Task Force
  on Recruitment & Retention Issues, a subcommittee of the Association of College & Research Libraries, Personnel Administrators & Staff Development Officers Discussion Group.
    p. cm.
  Includes bibliographical references.
  ISBN 0-8389-8209-3 (alk. paper)
  1. College librarians--Recruiting--United States. 2. Library personnel management--United States. 3. Employee retention
  --United States. I. Title. II. Title: Recruitment, retention,
and
  restructuring.
  Z682.35.R42A85 2002
  023'.9--dc21

2002010821

Printed in the United States of America.

06 05 04 03 02   5 4 3 2 1

TABLE OF CONTENTS

Preface

Librarianship is experiencing a labor gap between increasing demand for library and information science professionals and a declining supply of qualified individuals—resulting in an increasing number of unsuccessful recruitment efforts.

In response to these developments, the Personnel Administrators and Staff Development Officers Discussion Group of the Association of College and Research Libraries (ACRL) established the Ad Hoc Task Force on Recruitment and Retention Issues in early 2001 to examine how academic libraries can successfully recruit and retain professionals in an increasingly competitive environment. This white paper addresses the twin issues of recruitment to the profession and recruitment to academic libraries in particular and documents the topics of discussion, presents questions, and compiles various strategies for enhancing recruitment and retention efforts.

With the rapid rise in information technology and electronic information resources, the demand for skilled library professionals is on the increase. Several studies noted in this report have documented the decreasing supply of qualified professionals and identified several causes. Among the primary factors identified are:

- the aging of the general labor supply and of the library profession leading to an increasing number of retirements;
- one of the lowest unemployment rates in U.S. history;
- the flat or declining number of master's of library and information science (MLIS) graduates;
- increased competition from other career sectors (e.g., private sector, corporate libraries, technology and dot.com companies);
- less than competitive salaries;
- a lingering negative image of the profession.

The increasing demand for library professionals, coupled with the changing nature of librarianship, is beginning to impact the recruiting environment, which is likely to change dramatically and become increasingly competitive. Shortages of MLIS degree holders, increasing retirements, and low salaries make the supply–demand gap even greater for academic libraries.

Following a review of the current environment, the discussion turns to an examination of issues and themes and later to strategies for recruitment, retention, and the potential for restructuring library education and the library workforce. Recruitment to the profession will require the active participation of professional associations, library and information science programs, and individual libraries. Making a profession attractive requires a mix of the right ingredients—competitive salaries, challenging jobs, a growing demand for professional expertise, respect for the profession, and long-term opportunities for growth. More than ever, active marketing and publicity campaigns will be needed to spur interest in, and attract attention to, the career opportunities in librarianship.

Suggested strategies for professional associations include marketing efforts and media campaigns that promote the value of the library profession and of the graduate library and information science degree. Media campaigns and other promotional efforts might include public service announcements and advertising campaigns, along with job and career fairs that feature opportunities in librarianship. Such campaigns also need to target wider audiences (including younger groups such as middle and high school and undergraduate students). Library schools are encouraged to increase enrollment through more effective marketing by highlighting the flexibility and versatility of the MLIS, expanding and updating curricula, enhancing the availability of degree programs through distance education, and targeting potential students earlier in their academic careers (e.g., undergraduates, high school students, etc.). Individual academic libraries can enhance recruitment efforts by promoting their professional programs locally, partnering with other campus entities (e.g., career services), offering financial incentives (e.g., scholarships, work-study programs, internships, etc.), and targeting other local groups that would introduce librarianship as a career to younger people.

Other suggested strategies for professional associations include revamping placement services and employment Web sites, developing new recruitment and advertising models to take advantage of new electronic media, and establishing fee-based recruitment services. Library and information science programs are encouraged to poll LIS students about their interests in academic libraries, develop and offer internships and apprenticeships, and invite human resources officers and academic librarians to give seminars to library science students. Academic institutions and libraries have numerous opportunities for enhancing the effectiveness of recruitment efforts through more effective marketing of the benefits of the academic environment and a streamlining of the search process. Institutions are encouraged to consider geographic factors and promote the benefits of their surrounding community. Other suggestions include considering using the services of executive search firms, offering finders or referral fees to employees who refer qualified applicants, filling more positions with entry-level professionals, and providing opportunities for training and new skills acquisition.

Given the increasing difficulty in recruiting MLIS graduates to academic libraries, retention of qualified and motivated employees becomes even more critical. Understanding the needs of employees at the various stages of their careers, as well as the reasons for staying with a job or seeking a new one, is one key to developing retention strategies. Professional associations and MLIS programs can assist in this respect by conducting regular, periodic job satisfaction surveys that would help shed light on how and why MLIS graduates make the job and career choices they do. Academic libraries are encouraged to examine individual employee needs and consider such retention factors as salary and benefits, position responsibilities, opportunities for growth and development, opportunities for advancement and promotion, quality of work life, and relationships with supervisor and colleagues.

Retention strategies fall into several general categories: salary and other compensation, working conditions, enrichment, and education. Improving working conditions might include creating new and more interesting job duties, providing opportunities for job rotation or exchange or job sharing, or allowing for more flexible work schedules. Professional development and educational opportunities can also be very effective in retaining top employees and enhancing individual job performance. Other recommended strategies include making counteroffers (both in terms of salary and other nonsalary considerations, such as travel funds, flexible schedules, research leave, etc.). It is also important to maintain a strong supportive environment, with abundant mentoring, to help maximize opportunities for success.

Restructuring both library education and the library workforce are also vital to meeting the ongoing needs of the profession in the midst of dramatic change. Although there is general agreement that the MLIS will remain a valued and essential credential, it is also recognized that it may be necessary to more broadly consider alternatives for some types of library work. These alternatives might include non-MLIS functional specialists (e.g., computer, accounting, human resources specialists), entry-level professionals with bachelor's degrees in information science, and other education/degree combinations and models.

In order to more effectively restructure library education, library educators need to have more interaction with library employers about needs. Library schools are encouraged to survey library employers on a regular basis and to work with professional organizations to establish formal continuing education systems and credentialing. Placement officers are encouraged to work more closely with human resources officers in academic libraries to facilitate placement.

Acknowledgments

This report is the result of the efforts of a number of individuals, and we would like to thank them for their time and contributions in developing this book.

First and foremost, we would like to thank the members of the Ad Hoc Task Force on Recruitment and Retention Issues, a subcommittee of the Association of College and Research Libraries' Personnel Administrators and Staff Development Officers Discussion Group, who worked on this report and were critical to development of its content and focus. The members of the task force were:

> William Black, Middle Tennessee State University;
> Kathleen DeLong, University of Alberta;
> Ken Hood, University at Buffalo;
> Kurt Murphy, Arizona State University;
> Carol Olsen, Stanford University;
> Laine Stambaugh, University of Oregon;
> Teri R. Switzer, Auraria Library/University of Colorado-Denver;
> Diane Turner, Yale University;
> Denise Weintraub, University of Chicago.

We would also like to extend our thanks to Jennifer Sweeney, former library analyst at the University of California at Davis, for her efforts in researching and reviewing the literature to prepare both a literature review and an annotated bibliography for this publication.

In addition, we would like to express appreciation to the following individuals who reviewed and edited the report at various stages and assisted in moving this project toward publication:

> Mary Ellen Davis, Association of College and Research Libraries;
> Hugh Thompson, Association of College and Research Libraries;
> Mary Jo Lynch, American Library Association;
> DeEtta Jones, Association of Research Libraries.

Finally, we would like to express our appreciation to the members of the ACRL Personnel Administrators and Staff Development Officers Discussion Group for their support, interest, contributions, and, most important, for their willingness to share their professional expertise. We thank them for their time, energy, and thoughtful deliberations on these issues.

George Bynon, University of California at Davis
Pat Hawthorne, University of California at Los Angeles
Cochairs, Ad Hoc Task Force on Recruitment and Retention Issues
May 20, 2002

Introduction

The fundamental labor problem is that there are fewer people to fill jobs.
We cannot do business as usual.

Such are among the statements of human resources officers in academic libraries of various sizes from throughout the United States. In Canada, the situation is somewhat different.

Something is happening as library search committees and supervisors seek to attract and hire qualified candidates for positions at all levels. Anecdotally, human resources officers can tell you the impact of a changing labor market, of increased demand and a declining supply of applicants—smaller and shallower pools of applicants, an increasing number of unsuccessful searches, candidates declining offers to take other jobs (some outside libraries), multiple searches for the same position, losing candidates to other libraries or employers when the search process takes a long time, larger numbers of vacancies, the increased stress on existing workers who must take on additional duties, and the inability to do all that needs to be done when a workforce is fewer in number than needed.

Participants in the Personnel Administrators and Staff Development Officers Discussion Group of the Association of College & Research Libraries have been meeting at each annual conference and annual midwinter meeting of the American Library Association for a number of years. Each meeting provides practitioners with a multitude of sound professional advice provided by experts willing to share their experience and knowledge, successes and failures. In the past year or two, the tenor of those conversations has changed as more and more libraries are experiencing a changing and contracting labor market.

In the past two years, the conversation has returned time and again to recruitment and retention and the difficulty more and more of our libraries are facing in recruiting and retaining librarians. Dire predictions of huge numbers of retirements and the flat or declining number of library and information science graduates are creating a dilemma, one that seems destined to have serious ramifications for the profession over the next two decades.

The central question: *How can we competitively and successfully recruit and retain those professionals needed in academic libraries for the future?*

At the ALA Midwinter Meeting in Washington, D.C., in January 2001, the twin issues of recruitment to the profession, and to academic libraries in particular, and retention were discussed at the ACRL Personnel Officers and Staff Development Officers Discussion Group on January 13 and 14, 2001.

On both Saturday and Sunday morning, various strategies and issues related to the ability to recruit were discussed including: getting large pools or even adequate pools for a position, competing with IT companies, salary and compensation issues, requiring the MLIS versus not requiring it, etc. Retention issues also emerged in the discussion related to the competition from IT and dot.com companies and the strong economy (something that has changed following the events of September 11). The declining number of MLIS graduates was another topic. The wide variety of issues and strategies being employed to address recruitment and retention issues led to more discussion of the overall issue of long-term recruitment given the expected number of retirements and fewer graduates (smaller library and information science enrollments, shrinking pools, competition from nonlibrary organizations, etc.).

Because of the importance of this issue, George Bynon of the University of California at Davis suggested that the larger discussion group membership consider appointing a small ad hoc task force and charge it to develop a white paper on recruitment and retention issues in academic librarianship. Based on the discussion at the meetings, many felt this was a worthwhile project to help us and others in the profession gain a better understanding of the issues and trends and to develop both short- and long-term strategies for addressing the problem.

Cochaired by George Bynon (University of California at Davis) and Pat Hawthorne (University of California at Los Angeles), the ad hoc task force included: William Black (Middle Tennessee State University), Kathleen DeLong (University of Alberta), Ken Hood (University at Buffalo), Kurt Murphy (Arizona State University), Carol Olsen (Stanford University), Laine Stambaugh (University of Oregon), Teri R. Switzer (Auraria Library/University of Colorado-Denver), Diane Turner (Yale University), and Denise Weintraub (University of Chicago).

The charge of the ad hoc task force was to address the issue of how we can "competitively and successfully recruit and retain those professionals needed by the profession for the future" and to develop multiple strategies—including radical ideas and new approaches—that might be used by the profession at large, library schools, and individual institutions. (For the complete charge of the ad hoc task force, see appendix A.)

I. THE CURRENT ENVIRONMENT

Librarians, long seen as members of a dry and dusty profession that is out of tune with modern times, are suddenly in demand. Part of the reason lies in the rapid rise of information technology. Library science graduates are now courted for jobs as database managers, Webmasters, or information network administrators— as well as more traditional jobs, according to a recent report by the U.S. Bureau of Labor Statistics.

"Librarians in Demand as Job Needs Change"
Boston Globe, January 22, 2001

The source of the *Boston Globe* article quoted above was the publication of a Bureau of Labor Statistics report early in 2001 on the job prospects for librarians. The BLS report details the job prospects for librarians in the winter 2000–2001 issue of *Occupational Outlook Quarterly* in an article entitled "Librarians: Information Experts in the Information Age" (Crosby 2000–2001). According to Crosby, the number of librarian jobs is expected to increase by about 5 percent (about 7,000 more jobs in 2008 than in 1998) and many experienced librarians are expected to retire, switch to another occupation, or leave the profession for other reasons by 2008, thus creating about 39,000 job openings for new librarians between 1998 and 2008.

While the BLS report predicts that the majority of librarian job openings will continue to be in public libraries, schools, colleges, and universities, it points out that the increasing technological expertise and skills of library and information science graduates make librarians more marketable and that "librarian employment growth is expected to be faster in other settings, including businesses" (Crosby 2000–2001).

The *Boston Globe* article points out that in recent years the number of annual retirements has been double the number of graduates coming out of library and information science programs. Librarians are being heavily recruited by the private sector and going to work in nonlibrary settings, and this competition is resulting in increased salaries in a profession that has not been highly paid. "In 1998, librarians earned an average of $40,020, about a 5 percent increase over 1997 earnings, according to the BLS." Starting salaries rose more than 5 percent in 1998 for librarians compared to 4 percent growth for salaries for all technical, professional, paraprofessional, and managerial workers (Crosby 2000–2001).

Crosby's article in *Occupational Outlook Quarterly* and the *Boston Globe* article illustrate the growing demand for the professional expertise and skills of librarians in both traditional library settings and new nonlibrary settings. As the demand grows, the profession is beginning to step up its effort to recruit more individuals to library careers in an effort to meet what will become a growing demand for librarians who hold the MLIS degree.

ALA president John W. Berry was interviewed by the *Indianapolis Star* about the demand for librarians and ALA's newly launched public relations campaign to improve the image of the profession and recruit more librarians (Weaver 2001). In this article, Berry cites some of the major reasons for the shortage of librarians:

• *Lack of new blood:* With the numbers of MLIS graduates increasing only slightly, there are just not enough graduates to keep up with the increased demand.

• *Low salaries:* Among careers requiring master's degrees, librarians earn an average starting salary of $31,915 (in 1998) compared to $50,000 starting salaries for advanced degrees in marketing, nursing, or computer engineering. Although librarians' salaries are increasing, they would need to increase dramatically to be equal to salaries in positions requiring comparable graduate education. Low salaries within the profession make the profession less attractive.

- *Increased competition*: Low pay at public and school libraries is leading some MLIS graduates and experienced librarians to opt for higher-paying jobs in the private sector, in corporate libraries or with technology or, dot.com companies.

Berry made recruitment to the profession one of the themes of his ALA presidency, along with diversity. In April 2002, ALA hosted a national town hall meeting—"Recruitment @ Your Library"—to bring national attention to the value of human resources to educational institutions such as libraries.

On January 9, 2002, First Lady Laura Bush, a former librarian, announced a new $10 million initiative to be funded in President George W. Bush's fiscal 2003 budget. Managed by the federal Institute for Museum and Library Services (IMLS), the multimillion-dollar initiative will fund a variety of programs to recruit librarians, including scholarships for graduate students in library and information science, distance learning technology for training programs in underserved areas, and recruitment of librarians with diverse language skills.

Such recent publicity in the popular media is echoing what has been emerging in the professional literature and is becoming a hot topic—again. "In the last 40 years, librarianship has had three periods of shortages and two corresponding periods of what appeared to be an oversupply of professional librarians" (Matarazzo 1989). According to Matarazzo, the first oversupply of librarians occurred in the 1970s and was well documented in the 1975 Bureau of Labor Statistics (BLS) study, *Library Manpower: A Study of Demand and Supply*. A second major report, *Library Human Resources: A Study of Supply and Demand*, was published in 1982 by King Research for the National Center for Educational Statistics and the Office of Library and Learning Technologies. The King research study described a declining number of MLIS graduates and predicted modest increases in job vacancies through 1990. Although the study was extensive and comprehensive in its analysis of data, Matarazzo asserts it was flawed in that the data used did not include the most up-to-date statistics at the time, the 1980 census. Using the 1980 census data that were not used in the King research study, Matarazzo confirmed there were nearly 50,000 more librarians working than indicated in the data used in the King study. Yet the most critical data element missing in the King study was the probable number of retirements. Matarazzo's research illustrated that this was a key bit of information—between 1980 and 2000, approximately 70,000 librarians would reach retirement age and would retire or leave the profession for other reasons. Given the more up-to-date statistics, what began to emerge was an increasing number of vacancies (due to retirements and departures from the profession) at the same time the King study had indicated that a surplus of librarians would exist.

By the mid-1980s, Matarazzo noted that library and information programs were seeing increased numbers of vacancies and activity in their placement centers whereas the number of MLIS graduates remained relatively flat.

In the March 2002 issue of *American Libraries*, Mary Jo Lynch's article, "Reaching 65: Lots of Librarians Will Be There Soon," pointed out that it is difficult to accurately predict retirements given that retirement is such a personal decision, but that it is *not* difficult to estimate the number of librarians who will reach age 65 over the next 30 years. Using 1990 census data, Decision Demographics' analysis showed that approximately 10 percent of 87,409 librarians will reach age 65 between 2000 and 2004, 16 percent between 2005 and 2009, more than 20 percent between 2010 and 2014, and approximately 18 percent between 2015 and 2019. This means that more than 60 percent of librarians currently employed will reach retirement age by 2020. Although not all will retire at age 65, the volume of potential retirements illustrates the need to increase the number of MLIS graduates and other professionals to fill positions vacated by this large number of retirements.

Knowing that the profession has experienced both shortages and oversupplies of librarians over the past several decades is the first step in gathering information about the labor market. Examining specific information about each cycle of shortage or oversupply is the second step in developing an understanding of how the profession's labor market behaves. Determining what external factors can and will impact the supply and demand for librarians is another step.

In terms of recruitment issues, we need to determine how much of the current situation is cyclical and how much is part of a major fundamental and systemic change. Both the 1975 BLS study and the 1982 King study include the kind of data on projected retirements, departures from the profession, and MLIS graduates that can be analyzed to determine supply and demand and create projections. With such data available, it seems that regular analysis of such projections and trends would be beneficial to the profession at large and may be a task best undertaken by ALA and the other major professional library associations.

As we head into what appears to be another shortage of librarians in a time of economic uncertainty, many questions come to mind. Will the economic downturn exacerbated by the events of September 11 lead to increased graduate school enrollments? Will jobs be cut from libraries? How will layoffs now affecting the private sector impact library recruiting? Will librarians in private-sector or nonlibrary settings seek out jobs in traditional libraries? Will the shortage of librarians in the next decade continue to drive up salaries? If so, will higher salaries attract more applicants to MLIS programs as research has indicated? If we are successful in attracting more individuals to MLIS programs, will the pendulum swing in the other direction and will an oversupply of librarians then exist? What changes are permanent? Will the pendulum swing back and, if so, when?

To be able to answer such questions, we need to understand the nature of the current labor market and projections related to our profession and be able to determine the characteristics of the population of working librarians, specifically those in academic libraries. We need to understand the shortages within specific types of libraries and in individual libraries so that differences and similarities can be identified.

The Age Demographics of Academic Librarians: A Profession Apart (Wilder 1995) offers a picture of what lies ahead for academic libraries. Examining data from the Association of Research Libraries Annual Salary Surveys for 1990 and 1994, Wilder determined that "as a group, librarians, including those who work in Association of Research Libraries (ARL) member libraries, are older than members of most comparable professions, and the group is getting older."

When compared to similar professions, librarianship has only about half the number of individuals aged 30 and under that other professions have and 40 percent more individuals aged 45 or older (Wilder 1995). Some of this may be due to the fact that many come to the profession as a second career. The reality of this fact is that someone who enters the profession at 45 years of age, as opposed to entering the profession at the age of 25, will have fewer career years in the library labor force.

Wilder found that the average age of U.S. librarians was stable between 1970 and 1990, but that between 1990 and 1994, librarians as a population aged rapidly. "In 1990, 48 percent of librarians were aged 45 and over, compared with 58 percent in 1994" (Wilder 1995). The dramatic shift in this professional population could not be attributed to the aging of the population in general. The rapid aging of academic librarians was an anomaly when compared to other comparable professional groups.

Wilder identified several factors that contributed to the dramatic shift, including:

- Librarians aged 35 and under are generally underrepresented in the profession. Individuals aged 25 to 34 make up 14 percent of the librarian population, but 27 percent, almost double, the population of those in the professional specialty categories (the comparable professions to which Wilder compared librarianship in the *Current Population Survey* (CPS) data.

• Between 1990 and 1994, the librarian population aged rapidly in a relatively short period of time. The "aging" of this population "appears to be a function of the steady increase in the portion of the population in the 45 to 54 age group combined with a nearly corresponding decline in the 35 to 44 age group." Individuals in the 35 to 44 age group moved into the 45 to 54 range and "carried the apex of both distributions with them."

• One explanation for the trend can be attributed to the fact that the age of library and information science students increased sharply in the 1980s— the percentage of students aged 35 and over rose from 25 percent in 1981 to 50 percent in 1994. Unlike comparable professions where individuals enter in their 20s, many library and information science students continue to be older and pursue librarianship as a second career. According to the statistics provided by ALISE for the fall of 1999 (ALISE 2000) only 23.7 percent of students were aged 25 to 29 (although the data are incomplete).

• The demographic profile of academic librarians—specifically, the shape and movement of the ARL age curve—centers on the predominance of a single age group, Wilder notes, the group now aged 40 to 54, which consists of librarians hired in large numbers in the 1960s to service the baby boom expansion in higher education and the baby boomers themselves. This group stands out significantly because the rate of hires declined after 1971. "As this group ages through the ARL library population, the age distribution (the curve) moves with it."

• Another reason behind the movement of the curve in Wilder's study can be attributed to the reduction in new hires, from 15 percent in 1990 to 10.8 percent in 1994. When the librarians in the 40 to 44 age group moved to the 45 to 49 age cohort, the curve moved with them because of the reduced number of new hires. ARL libraries last hired large numbers of librarians in the 1960s and early 1970s.

Wilder's study defines many of the issues facing the academic library profession in terms of human resources. Using the ARL salary survey data to create retention tables and projections, Wilder (1995) determined that "retirements will have an enormous impact on ARL libraries over the next 25 years."

Wilder predicted that "16 percent will retire between 2000 and 2005, and 24 percent between 2005 and 2010. Between 2010 and 2020, 27 percent of the ARL population will retire." That means that by the end of this decade, 40 percent of ARL librarians could retire and 67 percent by the end of the next decade.

Many academic libraries in the United States are beginning to experience such waves of retirements. Colorado State University, for example, has had 25 percent of its librarians retire in the past six years.

When libraries in the United States began to experience higher rates of retirements in the late 1990s, major recruitment efforts began. In Canada, retirements took place, but recruitment efforts were not as robust. Volatile budget environments and major cuts in operating expenditures were common in Canada throughout the decade. Many Canadian libraries were forced to give up positions in order to fund budget cuts, to keep positions open, or to fund only temporary or contract appointments as service demands warranted. Few positions were filled on a permanent basis except for those deemed highly strategic (e.g., IT librarians). Some Canadian librarians speak of the "lost generation of library school graduates," those graduates of MLIS programs who drifted from contract to contract or moved out of Canada to practice their profession. As a result, many U.S. libraries enjoy the talents of Canadian library school graduates.

The situation in Canada showed little change at the beginning of 2002. Some institutions report problems filling middle-management positions, as so few were hired in the 1990s that management experience was not easily gained. Many institutions are expecting further budget cuts. Retirements are slated to occur, but permanent tenure-track positions will not automatically be filled. Besides the obvious problems of this continued downturn, such as meeting service demands and covering the subject and language specialties needed for building research-level collections, Canadian human resources librarians worry that their organizations are losing the vitality that new recruits bring to a professional group. Practicing librarians feel that few are following behind to maintain the legacy, whether of service quality or of collection strength, that they have built and fostered. As the rate of retirement accelerates over the next decade, this situation must change. It is hoped that the same forces (escalating enrollments, need for professional expertise, etc.,) increasing demand for librarians in the United States will stabilize the professional complement in Canadian academic libraries.

Wilder and Matarazzo are among many to point to the large number of potential retirements and the resulting supply and demand issue that is beginning to emerge. Whether the fifty-six library and information schools can produce enough graduates is an important question.

The problem may be more severe given predictions of potential labor shortages for the entire country. The impending retirement of the baby boom generation workers is not just a factor for the library profession, but for the nation and the economy at large, according to a General Accounting Office report released November 16, 2001.

Using census data and Bureau of Labor Statistics projections, the GAO report states that the "total labor force growth will slow from an average annual rate of 1.1 percent between 1990 and 2000 to an annual rate of 0.7 percent between 2000 and 2025" (GAO 2001). The report, *Older Workers: Demographic Trends Pose Challenges for Employers and Workers,* notes:

> The number of older workers will grow substantially over the next two decades, and they will become an increasingly significant proportion of all workers. According to the CPS (Current Population Survey), there were 18.4 million workers over age 55 in the labor force in 2000, a number that BLS (Bureau of Labor Statistics) projects to be 31.9 million by 2015. This expected increase is a consequence of both the aging of the baby boom generation and a general trend in greater labor force participation among older persons. Thirty percent of all persons over age 55 participated in the labor force in 2000 and, according to BLS projections, this percentage is expected to rise to 37 percent by 2015. If these projections prove accurate, older workers will comprise nearly 20 percent of the total labor force by 2015. Older workers are employed in a diverse group of occupations but are more likely than younger workers to be white-collar managers or professionals. Our projections suggest that older workers will become an increasing proportion of some occupations. For example, from 2000 to 2008 the percent of teachers older than 55 will increase from 12 percent to 18 percent. Due to an increase in full-time employment and a change in the composition of the older workforce toward white-collar jobs, older workers have experienced substantial real earnings increases from 1989 to 1999 compared with younger workers. Over this period, earnings increased by an aggregate 11 percent for workers age 55 to 74 compared with a 2 percent gain for workers age 40 to 54.

In its final recommendation, the GAO report calls for the relevant government agencies to "work together to identify sound policies to extend the work-life of older Americans, including those legal changes that would foster creative solutions to extending workers' careers," all to "address the potentially serious implications of the aging of the U.S. labor force and avoid possibly acute occupational labor shortages in the future."

Such potential labor shortages nationwide are likely to intensify the expected shorter supply of young people to enter the library profession and academic libraries. If demand for professionals rises in all fields, the result could be that librarianship may become less desirable, particularly if low salaries in library positions do not rise significantly.

With increasing demand due to retirements and the changing nature of our work, the recruiting environment is likely to change dramatically.

• The demand for higher salaries to attract individuals to the profession and to specific positions is likely to grow. If the demand to replace retiring librarians "becomes acute throughout the profession," Wilder (1995) notes, "salaries for librarians could rise relative to other professions."

• Excessive numbers of retirements may introduce more automation and increase outsourcing in individual libraries, particularly those unable to recruit professionals in adequate numbers to meet their needs.

• Potential labor shortages may encourage more employers (libraries and institutions) to provide incentives *against* retirement or incentives for retirees to remain on the job as part-time workers following retirement.

• Libraries are likely to increase the number of both professional and paraprofessional positions in public and technical services and further increase the number of functional specialists (professionals who are not MLIS librarians) in areas such as systems, human resources, budget and fiscal operations, and fundraising and development.

A labor shortage can be caused by demand increasing beyond available supply or as the result of supply falling below existing demand. Given the relatively stable number of MLIS graduates and the predicted number of retirements, our profession is likely to face a labor shortage that is caused by both increased demand and reduced supply.

The profession as a whole—and academic libraries in particular—are faced with the prospect of losing significant numbers of librarians as well as a tremendous amount of professional knowledge and expertise to retirements. At precisely the same time, the profession is also faced with an increased demand for the expertise, skills, and talents of librarians as the jobs of librarians grow more complex. In addition, higher education is predicting an increased wave of enrollments as the Baby Boom Echo generation reaches college age, a demographic tidal wave that is predicted to increase the demand for higher education and services within colleges and universities.

The emerging labor market is one that will be impacted by both supply and demand issues. Like the nursing shortage, the complexity of the labor market for librarians will need to be understood if we as a profession are to address the issues.

In the nursing shortage of the 1980s, the supply of nurses grew steadily to 1.6 million by 1988, according to McKibbin (1990). The shortage of the 1980s was not due to nurses leaving the profession or a decreasing supply but, rather, to increased demand for nurses in many settings (Kimelblatt 1989). As health care experienced numerous changes and became more complex in the managed care environment, hospitals needed more RNs than ever before and so did other health care providers. In the 1990s, all the standard economic responses to a labor shortage (increased supply, higher salaries, more RNs working, use of other health care professionals to lessen the demand) were in place—and still the nursing shortage persists (McKibbin 1990). The characteristics of today's nursing shortage—still front-page news—are different than the characteristics that defined the shortages of the 1980s and 1990s. But the end result is the same: no matter the causes or responses, the shortage is still impacting the quality of health care in the nation and is often reported as one of the major public health issues facing the United States.

The increased complexity of librarians' positions in libraries overall, and in academic libraries specifically, is also likely to increase the demand for more librarians as well as for additional professionals in other fields and more support staff. As the workforce changes, the distribution of work is likely to shift. As higher education prepares for the next wave of increased enrollments, one wonders if the demand for librarians will not echo the demand for nurses that began to increase as the population began to age and the need for health care exploded. Increased enrollments in higher education institutions is likely to lead to increased demand for library services and collections and resources as the demand for higher education rises.

With both supply and demand issues to be addressed in a rapidly changing higher education environment, recruitment, retention, and restructuring are likely to be major themes of the profession over the next decade.

II. ISSUES AND THEMES

Recruitment

Recruitment for academic libraries is an issue with three major facets—recruiting to the profession, recruiting to academic libraries, and recruiting to specific positions within individual libraries.

With more and more options open to women, recruiting to a female-dominated profession known for low pay and prestige continues to be difficult. The lingering negative image of the profession combined with low salaries (compared to other professions requiring an advanced degree) are systemic issues that cannot be solved by individuals or individual libraries.

The number of graduates, with ALA-accredited MLIS degrees, from library and information science schools remains relatively flat and fluctuates only a bit from year to year. Fifty-six library schools—forty-nine U.S. schools and seven Canadian—report student-related data to the Association for Library and Information Science Education (ALISE) annually.

Data from the ALISE Web site (http://ils.unc.edu/ALISE/) for total enrollment, total degrees awarded, and number of ALA-accredited master's degrees awarded for the past five years is outlined in the table 1.

Recruiting MLIS graduates into academic libraries and into specific libraries and positions is something that individuals and libraries can tackle to some extent.

		TABLE 1		
YearTotal	Total Degrees Awarded Enrollment	ALA Accredited (Bachelor's, Master's, Post-Master's & Doctoral)	Master's Degrees Awarded	
2000–2001	21,040 [+2,341 / +12.5%] Fall 2000 figures	*Data for 2000 – 2001 not yet available.*		
1999 – 2000	18,699 [-1,285 / -6.4%] Fall 1999 figures	5,999 [-72 / -1 %]	4,877 [-169 / -3.3 %]	
1998 – 1999	19,984 [+1,083 / +5.7%] Fall 1998 figures	6,071 [+236 / +4 %]	5,046 [+22 / +0.4 %]	
1997 – 1998	18,901 [-305 / -1.5%] Fall 1997 figures	5,835 [+125 / +2.2 %]	5,024 [-44 / -0.9 %]	
1996 – 1997	19,206 Fall 1996 figures	5,710 [-171 / -2.9 %]	5,068 [-203 / -3.9%]	

In a symposium on human resources sponsored by the Association of Research Libraries in March 2000 in Washington, D.C., John Lehner, the human resources officer for the University of Houston Library, outlined the factors shaping the recruiting environment for academic libraries:

- The United States is facing the lowest unemployment rate in its history (less than 4 % at the time). Each percentage point increase in the unemployment rate represents approximately one million jobs. In April 2002, the unemployment rate was 6 percent, an increase possibly due to the events of September 11.

- The number of librarians is declining. This is not the case in other professions.

- The number of library and information science graduates is increasing only slightly (approximate increase of 1,000 more graduates in the past ten years).

- The number of job seekers at the Placement Center at ALA Annual Conference and ALA Midwinter Meetings is declining while the number of jobs is increasing. In many cases, there are three times as many jobs as seekers. The end result is that the available pool of candidates/applicants seems to be shrinking. In reality, other factors may be impacting participation in the ALA Placement Center service. Job seekers and employers may not be using the service due to perceptions. Some employers feel the ALA Placement Center is not effective and do not post positions. Job seekers have the perception that many employers do not go through the ALA Placement Center or find it hard to connect with employers and tend to avoid using the center again.

• We are faced with rising demand and falling supply, which means higher salaries. Lehner cited the *Library Journal* Placement & Salaries Survey – the average starting salary for 1998 was $31,915, 5.4 percent more than the 1997 average starting salary of $30,270. (The trend continues. The *Library Journal* survey reported that the average starting salary for 1999 was $33,976, a 6.5 percent increase over the 1998 salary. And the most recent 2000 survey noted that the average starting salary was $34,871, an increase of 2.63 percent over 1999.) Yet these salaries continue to be lower than the average starting salaries for other professions requiring a master's degree.

• MLIS graduates are going elsewhere—to public, school, and special libraries and to nonlibrary settings in business and industry and to the private sector.

• Higher education is preparing for a new boom era between now and 2009. What are we doing to prepare? Will we be able to meet the needs?

RECRUITMENT TO THE PROFESSION

Recruiting to the profession is a critical need if academic libraries are to be able to fill professional positions over the next decade – and a shared responsibility. Professional associations such as the American Library Association, the ALA divisions, the Association of Research Libraries, and state library associations and organizations can play a role in recruiting to the profession. Library and information science programs also have a key role to play in recruiting to the profession. Individual libraries can also recruit larger numbers to the profession at large.

Recruiting to the profession will also require that we develop a stronger understanding of career choice, and of what leads an individual to select a specific profession, in order to capitalize on that information to market the profession in a variety of ways to as many audiences as possible.

Librarianship—like other female-dominated professions of teaching, nursing, and social work—has faced declining numbers as opportunities for women in other fields have increased. Limited opportunities for promotion in past years, low salaries, and a relatively poor professional image have *not* made librarianship a "hot" career. Demand, competitive salaries, and opportunities for growth are among the factors that help to make specific careers "hot"—whether the label comes from a government agency or an industry.

Yet tremendous changes are impacting libraries and the work of librarians—specifically, the increasing reliance on technology and the growth of electronic information resources. Now is the time to market the potential of the profession via national publicity campaigns such as the one recently launched by ALA. With @yourlibrary, ALA has the opportunity to stress the value of libraries as important and critical cultural institutions in the digital age where real differences are emerging between the technological haves and have-nots. Communicating the value of librarians' skills is another aspect. Even in the do-it-yourself-on-the-Internet society of today, librarians are needed to teach information literacy skills and to facilitate the development of problem-solving, critical thinking, and information management skills in an era where lifelong learning is key to success. The continuing importance of traditional collections and the roles of the library in terms of free access to information and as a place of community also must be communicated. Such national campaigns can increase the visibility of the profession but must be done with care so they do not replace the image of the librarian-with-the-bun with an equally shallow or misleading substitute. In a recent *Library Journal* editorial, John N. Berry (2001) calls on ALA to avoid "creating a new set of stereotypes" and, instead, asks that ALA "tell America and the world the real value of librarians and libraries."

RECRUITMENT TO ACADEMIC LIBRARIES

Within the profession at large, academic libraries specifically are facing a pessimistic recruiting picture. In the current environment, college, university, and research libraries of all sizes are reporting difficulties in recruiting.

In November 2001, the Office for Human Resource Development and Recruitment (HRDR) of the American Library Association conducted a Web-based survey of the members of the Human Resources Section of the Library Administration & Management Association division of ALA.

According to the preliminary report released for the ALA Midwinter Meeting in January 2002, ALA received 171 responses (84 of which were from academic libraries) from 644 potential respondents (26% return rate). The HRDR learned that 73 percent of respondents (125) reported difficulty recruiting MLIS candidates during the past six months. The top two reasons cited by the respondents were lack of MLIS degree holders and low salaries at their institutions. Some other reasons cited were a combination of factors or specific shortages (e.g., shortage of children's librarians). One of the survey's questions asked respondents to indicate what percentage of professionals in their specific institutions were expected to retire in the next five years. The responses were:

- 34 percent expect less than 5 percent of their librarians to retire;
- 22 percent expect 5 to 10 percent of their librarians to retire;
- 22 percent expect 10 to 20 percent of their librarians to retire;
- 22 percent expect more than 20 percent of their librarians to retire.

Individual institutions also face challenges in recruiting potential candidates to their particular school or library. Factors beyond the control of the institution or library—geography or cost of living or housing or requirements for tenure, for example—can negatively impact whether individuals will apply and who will apply.

In addition to the significant number of pending retirements, fewer library and information science graduates are selecting academic libraries as their intended career path.

Each fall, *Library Journal* publishes its annual Placements and Salaries Survey. Among the data reported is the total number of placements of MLIS graduates (as reported by the library schools who choose to report). Those placements are broken out by type of library or organization—public libraries, elementary and secondary school libraries, college and university libraries, special libraries, government libraries, library co-ops/networks, vendors, and a category for other. Table 2 details the total placements and the number of placements in academic libraries, along with the percentage of academic library placements and the annual change for the last six annual *LJ* Placements and Salaries Surveys (2,366 placements in academic libraries out of a total 9,532 total placements or 24.8% of placements between 1994 and 2000).

With the expected wave of retirements, attracting more MLIS graduates to academic libraries will require that libraries and institutions work together to sell the academic environment.

		TABLE 2		
Year of Survey	Total Placements for All Types of Organizations	Total Placements in College & University Libraries	Academic Library Placements % of Total	Change from Previous Year
2000	1,223	363	29.6 %	+1.7 %
1999	1,569	439	27.9 %	+9.1 %
1998	1,417	267	18.8 %	-10.1 %
1997	1,601	464	28.9 %	+5.2 %
1996	1,924	456	23.7 %	+2.8 %
1995	1,798	377	20.9 %	+6.1 %

Source: *Library Journal* Placements and Salaries Survey for 1994, 1995, 1996, 1997, 1998, 1999, and 2000. For complete citations, see references.

At the ARL Human Resources Symposium in March 2000, Lehner outlined three key issues to be considered in recruitment.

1.   **Geography:** Geography is important to applicants, and surveys and studies show that applicants "rule out" geographic areas. *Library Journal's* 1998 survey indicates that 65.9 percent of new graduates work in the state where they went to library school and 17.1 percent of new graduates work in a state in the same region where their library school is located; that leaves only 17 percent of graduates who left the region of their library school for a job. Yet most academic libraries automatically conduct national searches based on the faculty model. If the library or institution does not fund relocation costs, many librarians' salaries are not generally high enough for the individual to justify significant relocation costs.

2.   **Timeliness:** Searches and recruiting relationships need to be managed effectively. Searches need to be conducted in a timely manner. Keeping applicants in a state of limbo will not work in a market where competition will be stiff. Lehner pointed out that people remember the beginning of an employment relationship and may make judgments based on interactions.

3.   **Storytelling:** Rejected applicants can impact an organization with the stories they tell about their experiences. Libraries, search committees, and hiring supervisors need to consider an applicant's perspective on ALL recruitment activities.

Operating in such a recruiting environment will require academic libraries and their parent institutions to rethink the employment contract.

Understanding the needs of candidates is another aspect. Employers must determine what new MLIS graduates may be seeking in terms of mobility, opportunity, challenge, ability to use technology skills and learn new skills, and salary and benefits before they are able to even attempt to meet the needs of potential employees.

Smaller pools and the difficulty in identifying qualified candidates help academic library administrators show provosts and university administrators that libraries are in a competitive job market and librarians, like information technology professionals, can get more money in the private sector. There is no doubt that low and noncompetitive salaries hinder our ability to recruit and retain the best. Academic library human resources officers are in agreement that using the current situation to improve our professional status and salaries is both warranted and justified. Higher and more competitive salaries are only one aspect of recruitment—but it is a major one and is likely to grow more important in a tight labor market. Academic libraries also have to enhance and market the benefits of academe.

Academic libraries can assist each other by fostering placement. Some library administrators do not want to share applicants or endorse "recruiting from each other." Yet there are situations where organizations can and do capitalize on each other's needs. For example, library administrators may help a librarian moving to a new area for personal or family reasons by calling other academic library directors or writing letters of recommendation. Academic librarians—particularly human resources officers in academic settings—can and should find respectful ways to help each other out and to help place qualified applicants in jobs. Sharing knowledge about applicants who are qualified—but may not match our own needs—may help us to recruit and retain librarians in academic libraries rather than lose them to other settings. Finding ways we can work together to refer applicants and help place people in other academic libraries when we do not hire them can help us hang on to these applications.

RETENTION

Retention is the other side of the recruitment coin. Recruitment of top applicants and candidates may end with successful hires, but retaining qualified and motivated employees is a critical issue that will become more important for individual employers and the profession at large in the tightening labor market.

With a significant percentage of academic librarians planning to retire in the next decade and declining numbers of MLIS graduates and job applicants to academic libraries, retaining those current professionals takes on new importance. Such individuals not only need to be retained, but also need to be mentored, coached, and developed for future leadership roles in the academic library community.

Some individuals leave the profession or specific positions for personal reasons, and we recognize that in some cases these departures cannot be postponed or prevented. Focusing on retention practices for job-related reasons, however, is possible and should be the area of concentration.

Retention strategies generally fall into one of four categories: salary, working conditions, job enrichment, and education. Addressing these issues demands a specialized approach to developing retention strategies, or the reality is that academic libraries may begin losing talented employees to nonlibrary employers who can offer higher-paying jobs with better working conditions.

In some cases, retention strategies may even need to be customized to individuals in the tight labor market. Retention strategies need to differ for different stages of a person's career.

Individuals in entry-level positions or in the first five to seven years of their career are likely to seek jobs based on beginning salary, job duties, and potential to learn new skills or earn additional credentials. They may be more geographically mobile or open to moving for a specific position. Given the age demographics of the profession and geographic placement statistics, however, geographic mobility is not a given.

• Individuals in midcareer (7 years +), above entry level or perhaps in their first management position, may move for higher salaries or increased responsibility. In some cases, midcareer professionals may make lateral moves or return to the ranks after years in management. Geographic mobility may be more limited for personal or family reasons.

• Individuals beyond midcareer (15 years +) may seek new positions for entirely different reasons than entry-level or midcareer librarians. In some cases, these decisions may be based on lifestyle factors beyond the library's control (e.g., desire to work part-time, enter a different profession, travel, or to care for aging parents).

Individuals may consider any number of factors when deciding to remain in the profession or in a specific position, including:
• salary and benefits;
• position responsibilities;
• opportunities for growth and development;
• ability to move laterally to learn new skills or to make a career change;
• potential for promotion;
• quality of work life;
• relationships with supervisor and colleagues;
• work environment and image/reputation of the library and institution.

In order to improve retention, we will need to determine and understand why some librarians leave the profession. Specific libraries need to determine why individuals leave positions and their libraries. Exit interviews should automatically be conducted when an individual chooses to leave a position. Understanding these reasons is the key to addressing the issues and making changes.

Such changes to be made may include:
• working with institutions to systematically increase beginning salaries as well as salaries of current employees in order to remain competitive;
• advocating for improved benefit plans to meet the needs of employees and to provide choices;
• developing position descriptions that meet the needs of the library AND the employee;

- providing ongoing training and development opportunities both within the library and outside the library that benefit individuals in their current position and their future positions;
- creating new opportunities for employees to move within the organization, either laterally to learn new skills or upward into management;
- fostering workplaces that have a high quality of life and are stimulating work environments;
- creating multiple opportunities for mentoring.

RETENTION WITHIN THE PROFESSION

The variety of types of libraries within the profession can provide for unlimited professional growth and development—if individual libraries and hiring authorities are open to librarians moving between types of libraries. Yet many report that moving from public or school libraries into academic or special libraries is not easy or welcome in most cases. Providing increased mobility among types of libraries is one aspect of retention.

Another aspect is determining how many librarians leave the profession, at what point, and why. Several studies cite that nearly 40 percent of new public schoolteachers leave the profession within the first five years. Comparable statistics for librarians are not available.

RETENTION WITHIN ACADEMIC LIBRARIANSHIP

After individuals have been recruited into academic libraries, the goal should be to keep them. One major issue related to retention—and to recruitment as well—is faculty status. Discussed at some length, this issue seems an important one because it is the *single most distinctive aspect* of academic librarianship that makes academic libraries different from other libraries.

Yet anecdotal evidence is emerging that recent MLIS graduates and librarians new to academic libraries do not care to enter organizations where librarians have faculty status—or do not truly understand the variations in types of faculty status situations and avoid such environments as a result. Determining if faculty status is the reason why fewer and fewer MLIS graduates are selecting academic libraries may be of some importance to the Association of College and Research Libraries. Understanding the interests of MLIS graduates and what attracts them to public, school, and special libraries instead of academic libraries may be the key to developing effective marketing strategies to "sell" the academic library as an exciting and viable work environment.

The reality is that the need or desire for faculty status and/or tenure is mostly applicant driven—some candidates want it and some do not. Those who do not are likely to avoid academic libraries altogether or go to those academic libraries that do not have faculty status and do not require research. Those who do want faculty status will seek it out.

The debate among the academic library human resources officers is no different than any debate on the issue of faculty status. One view is that librarians should have faculty status because we are an active part of higher education and should contribute to the profession. A central tenant of this philosophy is that faculty status is about sharing professional knowledge. Some say that faculty status and research are of more interest to those with a doctoral degree. Others feel that librarians do not need faculty status, that a different type of academic status is more appropriate and has a value different from the value placed on teaching faculty.

Different colleges and universities have different faculty or academic status policies for librarians. Some, such as the University of Arizona, allow the library to define the criteria specific to librarianship. The University of Oregon has faculty status, but no tenure. Other universities, such as Vanderbilt, do not require "research" for reappointment and report it does not have a negative impact on retention. Whatever it is called, the ultimate goal is to have professionals contribute to the profession in some fashion.

Whether faculty status should be eliminated is not the real issue. Faculty or academic status is likely to be around as long as academic libraries exist—in many different variations. The issue then becomes, as it relates to recruitment and retention, how we inform and mentor and support librarians in such an environment— how we make this *single most distinctive aspect of academic librarianship* a selling point that makes academic libraries attractive work environments.

Clarifying expectations to candidates in the recruitment process is only the first step. After these professionals enter academic libraries, it becomes the responsibility of the librarians to create an environment that prepares, supports, encourages, engages, and mentors new librarians.

RESTRUCTURING

Efforts of individual libraries to recruit and retain librarians are not always successful. Increased vacancies and unsuccessful searches can lead to creative new strategies and models in an effort to staff libraries. Restructuring, in essence, begins when recruitment and retention do not meet the need. Many creative solutions—using the "whole bag of tricks"—are required to meet the needs of the organization and growing demands from constituents for services and collections. With restructuring, we are beginning to expand our concept of what the library's workforce will look like over the next two decades.

One of the ad hoc group's operating assumptions was that there ought to be alternatives to the traditional MLIS-need-only-apply model. There is general agreement that the MLIS as a credential is necessary and vital to the profession at large. The MLIS serves a unique purpose in that it defines our educational standards and provides librarians with the theoretical foundations of the profession. Given the needs of the profession and individual libraries and the number of graduates, it will not be possible to fill all positions with MLIS librarians. Individual libraries and the profession at large must be prepared to expand the library workforce in creative ways.

The expanded workforce concept will undoubtedly make our libraries look different, the end result being that we would definitely continue to need MLIS librarians (yes, perhaps even more of them) as we would also need more types of professionals (non-MLIS folks) to manage some aspects and more levels of paraprofessionals with different types of skills.

Within the Association of Research Libraries member libraries, one fundamental change has emerged (Wilder 1995) with the rise of the functional specialist. Academic libraries, for example, are now hiring computer information and information technology professionals in systems, accountants and financial professionals for budget positions, human resources professionals to manage the human resources function, and development professionals for fundraising and development. This trend, to some extent, mirrors what occurred in hospitals as the nursing shortage deepened—a wider variety of types of health care professionals emerged to take on more non-RN work from RNs (this freed up RNs for RN-specific critical tasks).

Another possibility that has emerged for consideration is to reintroduce the concept of the bachelor's degree in library and information science as an appropriate qualification for some positions or some levels of positions. This is now possible as the bachelor's degree has been reintroduced, and nine LIS schools now offer a bachelor's-level program. Many of those graduates, however, are not going into libraries when they enter the workforce. Yet this represents an entirely new labor pool that could meet some needs in academic libraries. For example, a bachelor's degree in information science combined with a subject major at the undergraduate level might provide adequate qualifications to serve as a reference or a cataloging paraprofessional or to manage units such as circulation, reserves, interlibrary loan, and document delivery. Those with the bachelor's degree might not be considered librarians or faculty, yet they would diversify the library workforce and would lessen the pressure and need for MLIS professionals at other levels.

A new educational model might also be considered—undergraduates in library and information science could be required to major in a subject area and get a minor in library or information science or information studies similar to teacher education programs that require undergraduates to major in a subject area and minor in education in order to obtain teaching certification. Another model that is analogous is that the bachelor's in information science could be to the master's in library and information science what the bachelor's in social work is to the master's in social work or what the bachelor's in business administration is to the master's in business administration. Such "continuum of experience" models could produce highly trained paraprofessionals while an MLIS could continue to be the necessary credential for consideration to librarian appointments and for leadership and management positions.

Even with hiring more functional specialists and those with a bachelor's degree in library or information science, the reality is there would still be a need and a role for those with the MLIS—particularly as leaders and senior managers. We will need to determine what positions absolutely require an MLIS librarian. What the library is doing is critical to the campus, so the MLIS is important to the vision and establishing the priorities. With a more diverse workforce, we will be required to define the term "professional" differently, perhaps more inclusively to value all the people who work in libraries, not just librarians. The goal is to staff our libraries with competent people. In considering different staffing models, we can achieve that goal and accomplish the work.

Academic library human resources officers are in agreement on one point: We cannot perceive a time when we will not need the MLIS, but we may also need other types of library employees who can enter our organizations and have opportunities and methods to move up a career ladder to professional positions, including librarian positions.

In some cases, jobs once reserved for MLIS librarians are now being filled by those with no MLIS—either those with a master's or doctoral degree in the subject area or high-level paraprofessionals. Formerly one of the "core" competencies, cataloging is a new example of work that may be done by paraprofessionals or subject Ph.D.s or, in some cases, is outsourced to vendors. In areas where there are deficiencies, such as collection development or information technology, for example, search committees and hiring supervisors may be willing to look at other credentials besides the MLIS to meet current needs. Insistence on requiring the MLIS may diminish as supervisors and departments want the position filled instead of having to carry the workload during the vacancy. Crisis situations may help to eliminate barriers and resistance.

In many cases, restructuring begins with individual positions. For example, Stanford University Libraries could not find a reference librarian to staff their information center. They redefined the position as an information technology position classified in a different pay band and had a great pool. A search to fill a collection development or reference position fails to yield anyone with an MLIS degree, and a new search is launched with modified qualifications that may now read "ALA-accredited MLIS or equivalent" or "ALA-accredited MLIS or subject master's," opening the search to individuals with graduate subject degrees and relevant experience.

Based on discussions of the ACRL Personnel Administrators and Staff Development Officers Discussion Group, many libraries are now using phrasing of this type in *some* position vacancy announcements. One issue is what is meant by "equivalent"—in some libraries, it means the foreign MLIS degree whereas in others it means equivalent education or experience. Determining when to require an MLIS, when not to, and when to open it up to equivalent degrees or experience, or require a different type of degree, varies by position and by library.

- Some libraries have not required an MLIS for a number of years. For example, the University of California at Los Angeles Library does *not* list the MLIS as a *required* qualification. Position vacancies read "such background will normally include a professional degree from an accredited library and information science graduate program"—the openness of the wording allows UCLA to hire people who may not yet have finished the MLIS or other graduate degrees that may be applicable to the position vacancy. Many applicants with the MLIS still apply and are hired. For UCLA, this has made recruitment easier and has not hindered the quality of the applicant pool.

- Stanford University Libraries is another institution that uses "ALA-accredited MLIS or equivalent" and defines "equivalent" as either education or experience.

- Yale University Libraries reviews each position vacancy announcement on a case-by-case basis and determines whether to require an ALA-accredited MLIS. If the job does not require it, Yale does not include the requirement. An example might be recruitment for an information technology professional (where a master's degree in computer science may be as relevant) or a finance professional (where an accounting degree or MBA might be more relevant).

Use of new language—MLIS or equivalent education and experience, equivalent library experience, advanced degree—is not widespread. It is usually by position and usually used on the second try after a failed search.

What is unknown at this time is how many libraries—ARL and other types of academic libraries—are hiring individuals into "librarian" positions without the MLIS. For example, Texas A & M University hires individuals with sub-ject-specialized master's degrees as lecturers who then serve as reference li-brarians for fifteen to twenty hours per week. Some may and do hire individu-als with subject master's degrees to do reference, instruction, and collection development work in a subject area; they are called librarians and enjoy the same type of position as librarians with the MLIS. Other libraries—due to faculty status, bylaws, guidelines, or union contracts—cannot hire someone without an MLIS into a librarian position or the librarian classi-fication scheme. For example, the University of Arizona requires the MLIS for librarians to be on the tenure track, but those with an advanced degree in a subject area and no MLIS are not in the librarian track and are on annual contracts.

Another complicating factor is faculty status. Librarians want faculty to see them as colleagues, so in many cases the subject master's may be as critical to the search as the MLIS and the conversation between a candidate and the teaching faculty is much more important.

Another factor to consider is whether using "ALA-accredited MLIS or equivalent" or opening up librarian jobs to those who do not hold the MLIS relates to diversity. If we do not limit our applicant pools to just those with the ALA-accredited MLIS, will casting a wider net get us larger and more diverse pools?

Debating whether to drop the "ALA-accredited MLIS" in advertisements for professional librarian positions has led to a spirited discussion with mixed views and concerns. Some feel the MLIS is critical and others do not. Does not requiring the degree devalue the profession and ourselves? One librarian noted, "Attorneys do not debate whether or not they need the JD."

One major point did emerge: There is a significant difference between say-ing we no longer need the MLIS and saying we no longer need the MLIS for specific positions (making the decision position by position).

Many of the human resources officers engaged in this discussion can agree that some positions in libraries may not need an MLIS; however, the MLIS still intrinsically holds value in several ways. Specifically:

- The MLIS may be the "union card" or the critical credential that pro-vides the foundation, specifically the conceptual foundation regarding values and ethics for the profession.
- The purpose and role of the MLIS remains and will continue to be more critical as we do more teaching and education.
- Hiring those without the MLIS requires that we must orient and teach them about the profession, our values, and our libraries.

RESTRUCTURING LIBRARY EDUCATION

Restructuring needs include library and information science education and must begin with more interaction between educators and employers about needs. Are programs providing the right type of professionals? Employers can best answer this question. Increasing the dialogue between employers and MLIS programs and educators is logical. Addressing this issue must go beyond curriculum issues to include accreditation and credentialing issues.

RESTRUCTURING THE LIBRARY WORKFORCE

Restructuring is leading many libraries to rethink individual jobs and job qualifications and requirements. Restructuring over the long term is likely to lead many of our libraries and our profession to have an expanded workforce concept—one where MLIS degree holders will fulfill key roles as leaders and managers, one where we have a more diverse and perhaps larger workforce in terms of numbers and types of professionals, and one where jobs and qualifications will be rethought on a regular basis.

Traditional thinking in libraries must be replaced with more innovative and progressive thinking that realizes:

• Jobs are no longer static. Professional roles and position descriptions are changing dramatically in academic libraries.

• Jobs require new skills and competencies. A librarian will have opportunities to learn new skills and to develop.

• Specialization in jobs is changing—functional specialists such as Web development or multimedia, subject specialists, etc.

• Professionals will need to practice continuous learning over an entire career.

• The librarian-to-staff ratio is likely to fluctuate and change over the next two decades.

In *Changing Roles of Library Professionals,* Janice Simmons-Welburn (2000) found that recent position vacancy announcements in ARL libraries showed a trend toward new skills—particularly technology and electronic resources experience and knowledge of educational, instructional, and teaching technologies. Simmons-Welburn's survey also found that most new types of positions were for electronic resources or Web specialist positions and for "information technology specialist" and "digital projects librarian." Many of the position vacancy announcements also indicated that the positions had been redefined to fit new organizational needs. Simmons-Welburn concludes that the "changing role of librarians and other professionals in ARL libraries are the consequence of new technologies and organizational development."

III. STRATEGIES FOR MAJOR STAKEHOLDERS

Addressing the long-term human resources needs of the profession cannot be done by individual libraries working alone. Preparing adequate numbers of professionals educated and trained in theory and practice and in the areas of specialization needed will require a joint effort on the part of all major stakeholders in the profession—professional associations, library and information science programs and educators, libraries, parent institutions, and individual librarians.

Discussions of the ACRL's Personnel Administrators and Staff Development Officers Discussion Group yielded numerous concrete strategies and practices currently being used by individual libraries as well as suggestions and comments that could be explored and implemented by the major stakeholders.

These strategies are compiled and organized as suggested strategies for each major stakeholder:

- professional associations;
- library and information science programs and educators;
- individual academic libraries;
- parent institutions (colleges and universities).

This list is not meant to be exhaustive; however, it illustrates the numerous creative responses to an emerging problem and, we hope, serves to begin a dialogue among colleagues.

SUGGESTED STRATEGIES FOR PROFESSIONAL ASSOCIATIONS

Professional associations such as the American Library Association, the Association of College & Research Libraries, the Association of Research Libraries, and state-based associations are key stakeholders in recruitment and retention efforts and in developing future leaders for the profession.

RECRUITMENT

• *Work together as associations to conduct regular surveys and studies of the labor force in libraries.* Two major studies of the library labor force have been conducted in the past thirty years—the 1975 Bureau of Labor Statistics study entitled *Library Manpower: A Study of Demand and Supply* and the 1982 King Research Study for the National Center for Educational Statistics and the Office of Library and Learning Technologies entitled *Library Human Resources: A Study of Supply and Demand.* These studies are decades old. Conducting such an extensive study today using all relevant data sources would help the profession to understand the demographics and the trends and what is happening to the current cohort of librarians. Given the predictions for waves of retirements in the coming years, conducting such studies every decade would allow the profession to monitor the demographic trends. A new comprehensive report may also help outline future needs in terms of projections for numbers of librarians needed in each type of library.

• *Continue the current ALA-sponsored media campaign* of paid advertisements and public service announcements to promote the value of the profession and the need for librarians and to enhance the image of the profession. Highlight the different types of jobs performed by librarians to get people excited about the variety of job prospects and possibilities in all types of libraries. Market the information technology aspects of the profession and the need for lifelong learning and problem-solving skills.

• *Get people excited about the profession of librarianship.* Consider public service announcements for television modeled on the current commercial about the young boy who wants to be a teacher and his father who wants him to be a doctor—and when the father asks, "Why teaching?" the young boy responds, "If there were no teachers, where would doctors come from?" Another idea for a commercial is to have a retired grandmother or grandfather sitting on the porch with his or her laptop helping his or her grandson find information to solve a problem—how did they do it? Well, grandmother/grandfather was a librarian for forty years. The value of librarians is that we can search the literature to find valuable information—use this in the publicity campaign.

- *Market the profession to high school guidance counselors, career counselors, and career coaches.* The more these individuals know about the profession and its prospects, the more likely they are to discuss career opportunities with students and clients.
- *Increase the number of scholarship programs* available for individuals to pursue careers in the field. The ALA Spectrum Initiative and many state professional associations offer a number of scholarships or fellowships to support graduate study. Increasing the number of scholarship dollars available and publicizing the availability in an aggressive manner can dramatically increase the number of applicants to library and information programs.
- *Use a high-profile individual such as Laura Bush or Bill Gates as a spokesperson* in the media campaign or in public service announcements.
- *Use the idea of testimonials in commercials.* Testimonials can come from new librarians and library users.
- *Begin recruitment to the profession early* by targeting undergraduates AND middle, junior, and high school students.
- ALA and other professional library associations should consider *using their annual conferences in cities around the nation to recruit to the profession* by sponsoring library career and job fairs—open to the local community and to library support staff in the conference city. Such career fairs should be marketed to two audiences: library support staff, and the general public. Library support staff members are often prime candidates to attend library school, and a career fair would allow them to learn about specific library and information science graduate programs as well as distance education options and scholarship opportunities. Opening such a career fair to the general public might encourage individuals who might not have considered the profession to learn more about the opportunities.
- **Develop new models to help academic library employers recruit.** Although the ALA Placement Center has become fee based and been revamped slightly, many employers report that it is less successful than it once was. Some of this can be attributed to the high numbers of jobs and low numbers of applicants. Some is also due to format. ALA should consider offering a type of electronic placement service that operates year-round, modeled on monster.com or other professional associations (Society for Human Resource Management, for example). In an electronic placement service, applicants could search by job type, geography, salary, etc. Employers should be able to view the resumes of applicants in the format needed or desired from the resume bank and be able to directly contact applicants. Use multiple models to attract different markets.

- *Explore different models and pricing structures for advertising* position vacancies in print and in electronic formats. Could *American Libraries, College & Research Libraries News*, and other publications offer a dual-pricing structure? One price for print, one for electronic only, one for both, and a combined price for placement in multiple ALA publications. *The Chronicle of Higher Education* offers a dual option. In addition, as a weekly publication, it has a short lead time for print advertisements and the advertisement also appears in the online version for one month.
- *Consider establishing a fee-based search service for applicants and for employers.* Offer total confidentiality for applicants. Although some private search firms exist, a search service affiliated with ALA, ACRL, or ARL could serve a purpose for applicants. Previous experiments in this area did not work due to the lack of confidentiality for applicants (i.e., applicants were reluctant to post their resumes in an open database that could be viewed by their current employer). This barrier needs to be eliminated.
- *Develop a comprehensive list of listservs and Web sites that can be used for recruitment of professionals and paraprofessionals.* Use listservs within the profession as well as more generic listservs and Websites such as monster.com.
- Work with human resources professionals in ALA and ACRL to *develop a comprehensive list of executive or professional search firms that work in the library and information science field* and make this list available to library employers.
- *Develop a Web site of recruitment resources available to all academic libraries.* For example, consider placing various search committee guidelines on the Web site so they can be accessible to other libraries.
- *Develop a Web site of links to various resources for potential applicants to LIS programs and to jobs.* Use New Jersey's "Become a Librarian" site (http://www.becomealibrarian.org/) as a model.

RETENTION

- *Determine how many librarians leave the profession for reasons other than retirement and determine when and why they leave.* The teaching profession often cites statistics on what percentage of new teachers leave the profession within the first five years. Comparable data are not available for librarians. If this is a part of the retention problem, surveys and other studies should be focused on determining when librarians leave the profession, and why, and where they go.
- *Survey graduates of LIS programs* to determine career plans, geographic mobility, job growth and changes, continuing education, and professional development needs.

- *Conduct regular quality of work life or job satisfaction surveys of members* to determine and track trends within the profession at large and by type of library. Gather information to help employers learn what candidates want in jobs.
- *Conduct exit interviews with those who leave the profession.* Finding out why people leave and where they go can be critical to retention efforts.

RESTRUCTURING

- *Encourage research and publication* on trends and changes in MLIS programs.
- Have associations such as the Association of Research Libraries develop *a meaningful salary survey and position analysis survey.* The language of the current survey focuses on an old demographic: librarians (professionals), support staff, and students. It would be far more useful if ARL or other professional associations could develop survey instruments that are on the model of a Mercer survey: content of job, qualifications of jobs, types of environment, salary, etc.

SUGGESTED STRATEGIES FOR LIBRARY AND INFORMATION SCIENCE PROGRAMS AND EDUCATORS

Library and information science programs and educators help to educate and train future librarians and leaders of the profession. Their contribution to recruitment, retention, and restructuring efforts can be enormous.

RECRUITMENT & RETENTION

- *Increase the overall numbers of students and graduates* to meet emerging and future needs.
- *Recruit undergraduates from all disciplines in more direct ways.* Target a wide variety of academic programs and disciplines. Market the flexibility and versatility of the MLIS graduate degree as attractive to any undergraduate major—make a point of highlighting the fact that a student can enter an MLIS program from any background with no prerequisites, unlike some other disciplines.
- *Expose undergraduate information science students and graduates to library employers and jobs* as well as to the nontraditional information science opportunities. Many new undergraduate information science programs produce students who never even consider library settings as potential career paths or employers.
- *Recruit undergraduates in information studies programs to master's-level programs* in library and information science. Promote the value of the advanced degree in the same field.

- **Recruit MLIS applicants and students from other careers that have applicability to specific areas of librarianship.** It is well known that many come to librarianship as a second career. Actively recruiting from targeted professions could increase the numbers. Some possible professions to recruit from include education and teaching, accounting, computer science, business, and management. Recruiting recent Ph.D.s in fields that do not have strong job prospects is another strategy.

- **Create a demand and market for the MLIS.** In recent years, the master's degree in business administration (MBA) has been one of the most popular graduate degrees around. How did this degree become so hot? How did the MBA become a job requirement? Who created the demand? The MBA demand increased because students wanted the degree in order to secure higher-paying jobs; starting salaries for MBA graduates remain healthy and the flexibility of the degree continues to make it an attractive credential.

- **Work with practitioners to expand the MLIS curriculum to reflect emerging needs.** The growing complexity of jobs within libraries may need to be examined to determine if the library school curriculum should be more specialized or if specific tracks should be offered (such as marketing in a business school).

- **Articulate differences between library science track and information science track and the job opportunities for students/graduates and employers.** Some academic programs are "library" focused; others are focused on information science and information technology. Some libraries feel that MLIS programs are no longer interested in producing librarians to work in their libraries. Finding a balance and providing students with information to understand the differences in career paths and job opportunities allows them to self-select.

- **Publicize distance education programs.** The lack of library schools in some locations represents a barrier. Graduate programs are being "packaged" in different ways to meet student needs—weekend programs, distance education via the Web, etc. Many graduate students are adults who are "nontraditional" students and may not be able to relocate geographically to attend an MLIS program.

- **Partner with and encourage strong library technician programs.** Many Canadian institutions offer library technician programs. Work with library technician programs to ensure that their graduates can work at uniformly high standards of paraprofessional work. Seek agreements that recruitment officers for library technician programs will stream their applicants to library school programs if qualifications are appropriate. Agree to do the same for applicants under qualified for MLIS programs.

- *Poll students in LIS programs* about interests in academic libraries.
- *Work with academic libraries in your state or region to provide more opportunities for internships and apprenticeship-type programs* that allow MLIS students to work in the various types and sizes of academic library settings while attending library school.
- Have your school *offer regular job fairs* and invite libraries of all types to be there as exhibitors.
- *Invite human resources officers from academic libraries to* teach classes or seminars or to lead job-hunting workshops or to talk about job opportunities in academic libraries.
- *Invite academic librarians to your library school for panel discussions or seminars* on the various types of faculty or academic status to increase awareness and understanding of MLIS students and graduates and to dispel the "myths" about academic librarianship.

Restructuring

- *Work with ALISE to survey academic library employers* on a regular basis to determine employment needs. MLIS programs often survey employers for accreditation reasons, yet many academic library human resources officers say they have little or no contact with MLIS schools about the needs they see emerging in jobs. Such surveys should be directed to the human resources officer.
- *Encourage placement officers to work more actively with human resources officers* in academic libraries to facilitate placement.
- *Work with professional organizations such as ALA's Congress on Professional Education to establish formal continuing education systems and credentialing.* Continuing education is more structured in professions such as law and medicine. With the tremendous change faced by library organizations, ongoing learning is critically needed to ensure that the profession and individuals can maintain long-term competency and professionalism.

Suggested Strategies for Individual Academic Libraries
Individual academic libraries are developing and implementing numerous creative strategies to recruit and retain librarians and are restructuring work within their organizations, which are undergoing tremendous change.

Recruitment

- *Do your part to recruit to the profession on your own campus.* Partner with other campus entities such as the career center to sponsor librarianship career days or volunteer to do presentations on library careers for your undergraduate and graduate students as well as faculty, staff, and the community at large. In the fall of 2001, the University of Miami Libraries and the Toppel Career Center cosponsored a librarianship career day event featuring presentations by the two Florida library and information science deans and breakout sessions with librarians from all areas of the UM libraries. Forty individuals from the campus and the community attended the event.

• *Consider programs to encourage undergraduate student workers to consider library science as a profession.* At Colorado State University, the library works with the student financial aid office to obtain "merit work study awards" for undergraduate students who express an interest in pursuing a career in library science. This helps the library directly because it expands the work study student base and helps the student who might not qualify for need-based work study funds directly. Securing a good job on campus encourages the student to consider the profession and helps to recruit to the profession.

• *Partner with academic departments to encourage undergraduate and graduate students in targeted majors to consider librarianship* as a potential career that capitalizes on their undergraduate or graduate study through work-study or internships or practicums—for example, accounting students can work in acquisitions, computer science students in systems or digital library programs, business majors in human or financial services, education majors in instruction.

• *Participate in campus activities that allow you to "recruit" younger kids to the profession* as early as possible. The University of Wisconsin-Madison Libraries play a role in every summer program for middle, junior, and high school students who might be participating in summer camps and programs or early admission programs, or who are being recruited to the university. The UWM Libraries offer a library education component and work hard to make it interesting, slick, exciting, and different because the librarians see it as a chance to recruit to the profession. In terms of human development stages and career choice, the middle and high school years are when adolescents begin to consider realistic career options. Providing information on the profession could have a payoff later.

• *Create opportunities that introduce librarianship as a career to young people.* Some librarians have invited Girl Scout or Brownie troops to the library to introduce librarianship as a career to the group. Be prepared to answer questions about the wide variety of job duties and possible career paths. Provide facts about earning potential at various levels in all types of libraries.

• *Work with school media centers and school librarians to encourage schoolchildren and teenagers to consider librarianship as a career.*

- *Partner with other libraries in your locale*—public libraries, school district media centers, special libraries, etc.—to set up a booth in the local mall during National Library Week to distribute literature about library careers and library schools. Offer participants a list of contacts they can pursue for more information.

- *Offer financial support and scholarships for support staff in your library to attend library school* through MLIS tuition support programs and stipends. Many academic libraries have "grown" their own librarians. Others such as the University of Chicago, use such programs to support individuals working toward doctoral degrees in subject specialties or systems.

- *Educate campus human resources staff, academic or faculty affairs staff, library supervisors, and search committees* on the current recruitment and retention environment in academic libraries and the needs of the library.

- *Understand and document both the direct and indirect or hidden costs of recruitment.* Determine the direct costs of turnover and recruitment. What are the costs of running a search three times versus using an executive search firm? Develop mechanisms to analyze the hidden costs of recruitment and vacant lines (stipends for acting positions, impact on morale, work not done, priorities not met, etc.). This is the NET DIFFERENCE issue. Human resources officers in academic libraries are encouraged to make university and library administrators and managers, as well as search committees, aware of these costs. In many instances, vacant positions mean lapsed salary money, which translates to available funds that provide budgetary flexibility for administrators. Trying to overcome this mind-set to show the true costs of turnover and recruitment may be difficult, particularly in organizations where salary savings provide the ONLY budgetary flexibility.

- *Work with institutional entities to simplify the processes for hiring foreign librarians,* for sponsoring individuals for long-term visas and work permits. Library administrators need to understand immigration laws such as NAFTA and institutional and agency procedures and processes to hire and retain foreign librarians.

- *Use new technology such as video interviewing or airport interviews to shorten the search process.* Costs may not be cheaper, but technology can save time. Investigate whether your campus provides such services or contracts for such services and use them to enhance and shorten your searches. Use technology to make searches and the interview process in-house easier.

- *Move from passive recruiting to active recruiting* by using executive or professional search firms, particularly for higher-level positions or positions that are difficult to fill. Using executive or professional search firms increases the pool and is likely to include people who may not be actively job seeking or "on the market." Enticing these "silent job hunters" can enhance the pools and increase the diversity. Kansas State University Libraries used an executive search firm to fill five positions. The firm identified 117 candidates and conducted preliminary screening, interviews, and reference checks and reduced the pool to seventeen applicants. KSU Libraries then interviewed five candidates and hired all five for the open positions. All this was done in 60 days for three of the positions and 75 to 90 days for the other two positions. The search committee was involved after the seventeen applicants were recommended. The search firm focuses on personal and institutional characteristics to find a match. Total costs were about $11,000 per person hired. Although these costs may seem high, many searches average in the thousands due to recruitment advertising and travel costs; comparing those costs to your average search costs may be eye-opening. The value of search firms needs to be discussed within the profession, with libraries and librarians that have recruited and been recruited, respectively. More information on libraries using search firms is needed—descriptions of the process and time line, advantages and disadvantages, experience of individual libraries, costs, and results. Many libraries find that using a search firm has a number of positives—the search process goes very fast, it entices individuals who might not be searching for a job or who might not have considered a specific position, it enhances the pool of applicants, the library experiences positive public relations, and search committee members think differently and may have a reduced workload.

  • *Work with campus entities to consider moving away from the time-bound recruitment process.* Widely distribute the position vacancy announcement and hire quickly—while still honoring affirmative action requirements. Many institutions still require placement of print advertisements and processes that add to the length of a search. Eliminating unnecessary steps or requirements can streamline the process and make it more efficient.

  • *Work with campus entities to identify and use the type of advertising that works.* If print is no longer relevant, convince the people who need to be convinced to drop it and use electronic means of advertising—electornic lists, Web sites, etc.

  • *Accept applications in electronic format as a way of speeding up the process.* Many libraries no longer want applications in print or via normal postal services. The University of Chicago states "electronic applications are preferred." Stanford University will soon require electronic submissions.

  • *Try new methods of recruitment.* Offer open houses for recruitment as hospitals do for nurses. Participate in job fairs at library and information science schools. Yale University Libraries are sponsoring job fairs at library schools in the northeast to attract librarians to Yale.

- *Ensure diversity of pools by expanding the recruitment methods used.* Libraries that wait to screen and interview applicants until they have a larger or large-enough pool run the risk of losing some candidates. Libraries can redesign procedures to tighten the recruitment process; however, they must still ensure that pools are diverse. This can be done by advertising in more places, posting the position on more electronic lists, etc.

- *Encourage department heads and search committees to be willing to consider and hire individuals right out of library school and to orient, train, and mentor them.* Do the same for librarians seeking to enter academic libraries from another type of library—public, school, or special. Be open to interviewing and hiring librarians from nonacademic libraries. Public, school, or special librarians have the conceptual background in library and information science and with orientation and training can make the transition to academic libraries. Avoid tracking or labeling someone as a "public librarian"—look for skills and qualifications. Many in libraries assume that after you start on a track (i.e., start in special libraries) you cannot switch over to academic and may not be welcome or seriously considered by search committees. Such thinking needs to be challenged in a tight labor market.

- *Look for potential in candidates and their qualifications* —stress this to hiring supervisors and search committees. Many within academe or search committees look a long time for the "perfect candidate." Train search committees and supervisors to screen applications effectively and identify the pool of qualified candidates (i.e., candidates who meet the minimum requirements) with potential. The next step is to encourage those hiring to interview and hire. Hiring someone who is qualified, meets the requirements, and has potential is preferable to not hiring while the search continues for the "ideal" or "perfect" candidate. Encourage those hiring to determine the ideal characteristics—potential, intelligence, skills, interest, enthusiasm, etc. Although no one wants to hire someone just to "fill the position," some searches bog down when search committees seek the "perfect" candidate and are unwilling to consider below their vision of "perfect."

- *Review requirements for positions before posting.* With applicant pools continuing to decline, consider each "requirement" and determine if it is absolutely necessary to the position. Do not require qualifications that are not absolutely required to perform the job (legal issues are one reason for this). This can increase the size of pools.

- *Take a serious look at the composition of the job.* Is it a challenging set of responsibilities that supports the requirements of an MLIS?

- *Support, foster, and develop internship and librarian-in-resident or residency or fellowship-type programs* that encourage LIS graduates to work in academic libraries and on special projects in academic libraries. The wide variety of these programs, which are becoming more common in academic libraries, is helping with recruitment and increasing the diversity in the profession. These programs increase diversity and draw more librarians of color. Some of these residency or fellowship programs carry a certain prestige and can help with recruitment. Any individual library can offer semester-based internships to LIS students as a method of introducing them to academic libraries.

- *Examine the search committee process and determine if it is the best model to use for librarian recruitment.* If it is, determine if your search committees are empowered to do it all. Determine what is required of the search committee—orientation and training, meeting with HR officer, meeting with library administrators to discuss recommendations, etc.—and decide what is minimally necessary. If search committees are not required for librarians, can hiring be turned over to the direct supervisors so that it is handled similarly to staff recruitment? Can a recruitment advisory committee model work more effectively?

- *Consider the composition of search committees to ensure diversity.* Include at least one person of color on every committee. Mix up the composition to reflect the makeup of your professionals—seniority, areas of specialization, etc.

- *Refine the search process and shorten the amount of time it takes to conduct a search.* Academic libraries, like their parent institutions, are notorious for the length of time it takes to conduct a search, especially when search committees are involved. Given the market and the possibility that top candidates will be hired quickly, human resources officers and librarians in academic libraries need to work to examine existing procedures and practices and refine the search process to whittle it down so that a search can be conducted effectively in three months or less.

- *Train search committees to begin screening applications immediately upon receipt and to move quickly* so as not to lose candidates to other employers. Searches need to be conducted in under three months. By tightening the recruitment process and shortening the time line, individual positions are more likely to be filled successfully.

- *Formalize guidelines and procedures for search committees within your individual library.* Think through the process and provide and ensure consistency. Avoid charges of disparate treatment and discrimination. Keep the human resources person involved throughout the search process. Search committees need to be able to work effectively and efficiently and quickly—make the necessary changes to make this happen—make the committee smaller, give it more authority, etc.

- *Determine if the search committee model is best for you.* Explore other models such as interview panels used in public library settings. Some of these models have immediacy built into the process and candidates get feedback quickly.

- *Develop a cohesive page on your library Web site to showcase information for potential employees and candidates* and feature links to institutional and library information. Pack the site with information and update it frequently to provide details on benefits and the institution and the library. Link to institutional resources such as the housing office. Ask applicants and candidates to visit the site to learn more about the institution and library prior to applying or interviewing.

- *Provide applicants and candidates with information about the community and its offerings.* Provide links on a recruitment Web site to local resources and information about housing, transportation, education, churches, recreation, art and entertainment.

- *Create a testimonials page from library faculty and staff.* Quote librarians and staff members about why they like their jobs or why they like working for the institution and the library. Encourage them to talk about the library's services, programs, and patrons. The University of Oregon Library has a Web site of staff testimonials for working in the library and living in the community; it is available at http://libweb.uoregon.edu/admnpers/whyaduck.html.

- *Involve teaching faculty in the search process to get input from users.* Invite key departments and faculty members to participate in interviews for librarians. Many librarian positions, such as subject liaisons or bibliographers, will interact heavily with faculty within a department. Involving that department in the interview process brings a user perspective to the search process and can be a very positive thing. The University of Oregon's search process is initially handled by the library; the initial screening is done and candidates are invited for on-campus interviews. Recognizing the time pressures on teaching faculty , the UO Library invites faculty to participate at whatever level they can. Some are appointed as full participants of the committee. Some participate as committee members only during the campus interview. Others are invited to attend presentations or special meetings.

• *Remind candidates and search committees that the interview is a two-way process.* In a tightening labor market, candidates have options. Search committee members can lessen the risk of losing potential candidates if they foster an environment that makes the candidate feel wanted and encourages dialogue.

• *Emphasize to everyone that how candidates are treated during an interview is a BIG factor* and can make a difference in whether they will accept an offer.

• *Consider keeping serious candidates informed of your progress.* Many academic libraries acknowledge that searches are lengthy processes. Some identify the serious candidates and keep them informed that they are serious candidates. This can establish a relationship and keep candidates interested. In some cases, candidates will communicate back where they are in the search. Some libraries report that candidates have "waited" out the process because of their interest in the institution, library, or position because they were informed along the way of where the search was in the process.

• *Analyze how unions (if they exist in your environment) impact recruitment for librarians and staff positions* and determine if the impact is negative or positive, then determine how to address negative factors and emphasize positive factors. The negative impact of unions may include job (work) and status protection that may be equated with an ossified workforce committed to numbers and an appearance on university committees.

• *Educate union officials on the issues hampering focused and timely recruitment.* Explore whether it is possible to relax or renegotiate contractual agreements that call for time-intensive processes (i.e., huge selection committees, extensive consultation with constituent groups, etc.). Seek their input as to how they can satisfy their needs for oversight or participation by designing processes that are both timely and rigorous.

• *Consider issues of geography and other factors such as cost of living* and how these might impact applicant pools for specific positions. Make changes to minimize these factors in the candidate's decision-making process whenever feasible.

• *Offer current employees finders or referral fees for recommending potential applicants and employees.* Some institutions will offer current employees a specific amount for each referral that remains employed for a specific amount of time, for example, one year. Stanford University, for example, pays an employee $750 if he or she recommends an individual who is hired and remains 90 days; the Stanford University Libraries match the $750, so a library employee can earn $1,500 for recommending an employee. The University of Chicago has a similar program.

- **Consider offering sign-on bonuses or incentives** to applicants for joining the library or the institution.
- **Offer student employees referral fees and incentives for referring potential student employees.** Stanford University offers a $20 café card for student employees who recommend other students as employees.

RETENTION

- **Create stimulating and exciting work environments.** Involve employees at all levels in this strategy.
- **Encourage librarians and staff to talk to their supervisor before looking for a job or moving on.** Creating an environment where staff can openly discuss their professional needs allows the library to restructure a position or make changes to meet the individual's need before he or she begins a job search or accepts an offer.
- **Coach supervisors to talk to librarians and staff about career plans and goals and job satisfaction on a regular basis,** at least annually during the performance appraisal. A supervisor who is aware of an individual's career goals and interests can make many small changes that can make a difference.
- **Consider counteroffers if you do not already** match salaries offered by other employers. Some libraries report that this practice is beginning to change. Libraries and institutions that have had long-standing policies not to make counteroffers are reconsidering given the recruiting environment. Educate your institution about needs and the market you face as well as the costs of recruitment and ask for financial assistance in matching offers from other employers to retain key employees.
- **Be prepared to make counteroffers to retain employees.** Counteroffers can be negotiated and may include more money or may focus on other factors. In some instances, counteroffers are not about salary only, but other aspects such as more flexible schedules, part-time work, new assignments, travel funding, research leave, sabbaticals, support, quality of work life, etc.
- **Create new jobs and responsibilities and change position duties,** as needed, to meet the needs and desires of librarians as well as the organization.
- **Mentor, mentor, mentor.** Create mentoring programs for librarians new to your organization, not just new librarians. Make it an expectation that supervisors mentor their librarians.
- **Rotate librarians among departments,** at least temporarily. Promote both short- and long-term internal secondary employment opportunities that

allow individuals to grow and learn new skills. Consider establishing entry-level positions and advertise them as jobs (similar to internships and resident programs that move the person through all units in the library). Allow the librarian the opportunity to work in several departments. For example, reference librarians can work in reference and government information departments and in branches as well as teach, and technical services librarians can work in multiple units such as acquisitions, cataloging, electronic resources, and systems. Provide new entry-level librarians with an opportunity to work in several departments and learn a multitude of skills. If not all librarians want to do this, offer it only to those who do on a volunteer basis.

  • *Establish job exchange programs* within your library and between your library and other departments on campus to allow professionals to learn new skills. Offer job-sharing opportunities among departments within your library. This can be done formally or informally.

  • *Be willing to change work schedules,* as needed, to meet personal needs (most places do this as a matter of course).

  • *Offer part-time or temporary work to retirees.* Many libraries offer such options to retirees in exit interviews.

  • *Consider encouraging people to postpone retirement or offer incentives for people to stay* longer if it fills a need.

  • *Provide an abundance of professional development opportunities* within the library. Allow and encourage employees to participate in professional development offerings on campus and in the local community.

  • *Offer opportunities to develop leadership* in overseeing individual projects and supervising project teams. Ask individuals to chair committees and task forces.

  • *Provide opportunities to participate in the organization at different levels* and in different ways. In other words, let people "make a difference" or "have an impact." Learn what that means for your staff and then let them do it.

  • *Send individuals for leadership training* outside the library and institution.

  • *Identify potential future managers and "grow" the individuals into future management roles.* Succession planning is more traditional in the private sector. However, many libraries will face the loss of managers with many retirements. Making sure that future managers are "in the pipeline" is critical to the continued functioning of the organization.

  • *Provide a variety of types of professional development funding* and create policies that allow the individual to select professional development opportunities. Use directed funding for specific conferences. Set aside funds for other types of professional development activities. Provide individuals with the release time needed to participate in such activities. At the University of Buffalo, the unit can provide release time and staff travel funds and the library provides matching funds.

- *Support professional development at higher levels* for more experienced librarians.
- *Support faculty status requirements with generous leave policies and funding.* Provide mentoring and support to make the experience a positive one. Faculty status and tenure can be a process that harms people or one that provides supports to ensure that your process is supportive and positive and recognizes accomplishments.
- *Use individual development awards for study leaves,* for example, $1,000 for travel and $4,000 for salary replacement while gone (paid by state at Buffalo).
- *Consider offering librarian or faculty fellowships*—$3,000 for research, travel, etc., funded by donors. This can be offered as a project-oriented competitive award. The University of Oregon Library, for example, awards up to two $3,000 awards each year funded through an endowment.
- *Have librarians present their research at faculty forums* as a form of recognition and to encourage other librarians to contribute to the profession.
- *Send specific units to retreats or field trips,* for example, send the whole Access Services Department to another institution to talk to their counterparts.
- *Conduct regular exit interviews to track why people are leaving.* Understanding the why may help you to address the issues.

RESTRUCTURING

- *Recognize that your library is likely to need and employ more types of professionals* than just librarians.
- *Consider the career development of staff with a set of guidelines.* Send them to library school while they work at the library and "graduate" your own staff into your professional ranks.
- *Monitor position vacancy announcements* to remain abreast of trends in position duties and organizational structure.
- *Establish core competencies* for all levels of staff.
- *Move your recruitment focus from position duties and requirements to competencies and skills* needed in your library. Interview for competencies, including the ability to learn new skills and a willingness to deal with change.

- *Create the next generation of leaders and managers for libraries through continuing education and training.* A training program at the University of Chicago has been designed to focus on innovation, communication, etc. (not cataloging skills). Leadership programs offered by parent institutions or professional associations can provide critical training for future leaders.

SUGGESTED STRATEGIES FOR PARENT INSTITUTIONS (COLLEGES AND UNIVERSITIES)

Parent institutions can also play a role in these efforts. In some cases, individual academic libraries cannot consider or implement some strategies given institutional philosophies and policies. Institutions that recognize the importance of libraries and librarians to institutional success and demonstrate the flexibility to remove obstacles and encourage creativity in recruitment and retention are less likely to experience difficulty in attracting and keeping qualified individuals to work in their libraries.

- *Help the library sell the benefits, tangible and intangible, of the academic environment.* Point out the intangible benefits of working in a college or university with faculty and students, opportunities to continue learning, etc.
- *Use current employees to "talk up" the benefits of working in the academic environment.* Use their comments as testimonials. The University of Oregon Library Web site features staff testimonials; it is available at http://libweb.uoregon.edu/admnpers/whyaduck.html.
- *Highlight benefits that are unique* to your institution.
- *Provide candidates with complete information about ALL benefits* offered by the institution in an attractive package via Web sites or brochures. Make these available to the library for recruitment. Many colleges and universities offer extensive benefits.
- *Be willing to move away from the time-bound recruitment process,* that is, allow the library to widely distribute the position vacancy announcement and hire quickly. Aggressive recruiting and flexibility can mean the difference between a successful and a failed search.
- *Enhance relocation programs to assist libraries.* Some universities pay for relocation. Others may not pay, but, instead, offer temporary loans or relocation services or offer discounts from certain movers. Include librarians in mortgage assistance programs that are available to faculty and other professionals.

IV. REFERENCES

Association for Library and Information Science Education. 2000. *Library and Information Science Education Statistical Reports: 1997–2001.* Available online from http://ils.unc.edu/ALISE/.

Berry, J. N. 2001. "Let's Not Trade the Old Lady with the Bun for a Bar-Hopping Airhead: Tell 'Em What Librarians Do Each Day." *Library Journal* 126 (17): 6 (Oct. 15).

Carson, C. H. 1996. "Placements & Salaries 95: Beginner's Luck: A Growing Job Market." *Library Journal* 121 (17): 29–35 (Oct. 15).

———. 1997. "Placements & Salaries 96: Counting on Technology." *Library Journal* 122 (17): 27–33 (Oct. 15).

Crosby, O. 2000–2001. "Librarians: Information Experts in the Information Age." *Occupational Outlook Quarterly* 44 (4): 2–15 (winter).

General Accounting Office. 2001. *Older Workers: Demographic Trends Pose Challenges for Employers and Workers.* Report to the Ranking Minority Member, Subcommittee on Employer–Employee Relations, Committee on Education and the Workforce, House of Representatives (Nov.). Washington, D.C.: U.S. House of Representatives. Retrieved on November 29, 2001 from: http://www.gao.gov/new.items/d0285.pdf.

Gregory, V. L. 1999. "Placements & Salaries 98: Beating Inflation Now." *Library Journal* 124 (17): 33–42 (Oct. 15).

Gregory, V. L., and K. de la P. McCook. 1998. "Placements & Salaries 97: Breaking the $30K Barrier." *Library Journal* 123 (17): 32–38 (Oct. 15).

Gregory, V. L., and S. R. Wohlmulth. 2000. "Placements & Salaries 99: Better Pay, More Jobs." *Library Journal* 125 (17): 30–36 (Oct. 15).

Group discussion (Notes compiled by Pat Hawthorne). 2001, July 31. University of California at Los Angeles Senior Fellows Program. Los Angeles, Calif. (July 31).

Kimelblatt, M. H. 1989. *The Nursing Shortage.* Washington, D.C.: AARP/Public Policy Institute.

Lehner, J. 2000. *Recruitment: Current and Future Issues.* Presentation at ARL/OLMS Library Human Resources Symposium, Washington, D.C. (Mar. 2).

"Librarians in Demand as Job Needs Change." 2001. *Boston Globe.* (Reprinted in *Miami Herald,* 22 January, 2001, 43.)

Lynch, M. J. 2002. "Reaching 65: Lots of Librarians Will Be There Soon." *American Libraries* 33 (3): 55–56 (Mar.).

Matarazzo, J. M. 1989. "Recruitment: The Way Ahead." In *Recruiting, Educating, and Training Cataloging Librarians: Solving the Problems,* Sheila S. Inter and Janet Swan Hill, eds. New York: Greenwood Press.

McKibbin, R. C. 1990. *The Nursing Shortage and the 1990s: Realities and Remedies.* Kansas City, Mo.: American Nurses Association.

Simmons-Welburn, J. 2000. *Changing Roles of Library Professionals.* ARL SPEC Kit 256. Washington, D.C.: Association of Research Libraries.

Terrell, T., and V. L. Gregory. 2001. "Placements & Salaries 2000: Plenty of Jobs, Salaries Flat." *Library Journal* 126 (17): 34–40 (Oct. 15).

Weaver, G. 2001. "Library Group Steps Up Recruiting Efforts: Image, Lack of Degree Programs in the State Contribute to Shortage of Qualified Librarians." *Indianapolis Star* [Indianapolis, Ind.] (July 30). Retrieved August 17, 2001 from http://www.starnews.com/print/articles/library30.html.

Wilder, S. J. 1995. *The Age Demographics of Academic Librarians: A Profession Apart.* Washington, D.C.: Association of Research Libraries.

———. 1996. "Generational Change and the Niche for Librarians." *Journal of Academic Librarianship* 22 (5): 385–86.

———. 2000. "The Changing Profile of Research Library Professional Staff." *ARL: A Bimonthly Report on Research Library Issues and Actions from ARL, CNI, and SPARC* 208/209: 1–5 (Feb./Mar.).

Zipkowitz, F. 1995. "Placements & Salaries 94: New Directions for Recent Grads." *Library Journal* 120 (17): 26–33 (Oct. 15).

Appendix A
Ad Hoc Task Force
Preamble and Charge

PREAMBLE

During the American Library Association 2001 Midwinter Meeting in Washington, D.C., the Personnel Administrators and Staff Development Officers Discussion Group of the Association of College and Research Libraries (ACRL) discussed the challenges associated with recruitment and retention of librarians and staff in an increasingly complex and competitive employment milieu. Specifically, the group noted several factors of concern:

1. the large numbers of anticipated retirements in academic libraries as the baby boomer generation exits the workforce;

2. the radical shortage of available, qualified replacements in an increasingly competitive marketplace;

3. the shortage of adequate numbers of graduates from accredited library schools;

4. the declining number of schools issuing the traditional MLIS credential;

5. competition from the private sector not only for potential employees with technical skills, but also for library school graduates;

6. the inability of academic libraries to compete with compensation packages offered by the private sector for prospective or current librarian and staff employees.

The ACRL Personnel Administrators and Staff Development Officers Discussion Group unanimously agrees that a creative rethinking of current recruitment and hiring practices would benefit and, ultimately, alleviate some of the employment challenges we currently face. To that end, an Ad Hoc Task Force on Recruitment and Retention Issues will be formed and asked to develop a white paper for consideration at the group's general membership during the ALA Annual Conference in San Francisco (June 2001) and the ALA Midwinter Meeting in New Orleans (January 2002).

CHARGE

Given continuing difficulties associated with recruiting and retaining qualified librarians and staff into the academic library environment, the Ad Hoc Task Force on Recruitment and Retention Issues in Academic Libraries is charged to:

1. Conduct a literature search for best practices in attracting, hiring, and retaining employees into the academic library milieu as well as a review of literature from fields facing similar issues (i.e., information technology, nursing).

2. Consider, discuss, and brainstorm any and all ideas that may serve to alleviate current recruitment and retention of qualified employees in the academic library milieu.

3. Draft a white paper that compiles best practices and creative ideas as outlined in 2 and 3 above and have it ready for ACRL Personnel Administrators and Staff Development Officers Discussion Group discussion during the Summer 2001 ALA Annual Conference in San Francisco and Midwinter 2002 Meeting in New Orleans.

4. Consider and integrate, as appropriate, comments received during the Summer ALA Annual Conference and ALA Midwinter Meeting discussion into the draft position paper and reissue it to the membership for additional and final comment.

5. Provide the final version of the position paper to the cochairs of the ACRL Personnel Administrators and Staff Development Officers Discussion Group upon completion.

In meeting its charge, the ad hoc task force is encouraged to "think outside the box" with regard to creative solutions and approaches to meet current academic library recruitment and retention challenges.

Appendix B
Literature Review

This document reviews recent literature on professional recruitment strategies in academic libraries as background for a position paper on that topic. The list of truly new or innovative ideas to increase the effectiveness of recruitment and retention as documented in the literature is short, but rich in potential. This review does not cover exhaustively the repeated calls for more and better public relations efforts, more action on the part of professional associations, and opening the professional ranks to credentials other than the MLIS. In addition, trends are only briefly noted with references to well-known surveys on retirements, salaries, MLIS graduates, position types, and changes in jobs in library organizations.

There are two new themes in the recruitment arena. First, the most visible and practical development is the burgeoning online recruiting industry, which presents significant opportunity for increasing the visibility of librarianship and the size of the professional applicant pool.

The second significant theme that affects strategies for developing new approaches to recruitment concerns the changing roles of library professionals and paraprofessionals in public services and technology positions. Similar to the shift in technical services staffing roles that began more than a decade ago, public services and technology tasks continue to shift from professional to support staff, including activities such as reference service, conducting instruction sessions, building Web pages (and contributing to content), maintaining computer networks, etc.

Effects of these shifting roles have begun to be reflected in recruitment and retention efforts. Some libraries have sent their paraprofessionals to library school. One health sciences library has instituted a new job family of health information analysts whose career ladder spans positions from entry-level paraprofessional to post-MLIS library science internships.

REVIEW OF THE LITERATURE
WHERE ARE ALL THE MLIS'?

Several issues surround the declining ability of academic libraries to successfully recruit professional librarians. Essentially, ballooning librarian retirement rates expected through 2010, coupled with a continuing low graduation population from MLIS-granting degree programs and noncompetitive salaries, has thinned the applicant pool of professional librarians in all types of libraries, including academic libraries (St. Lifer 2000).

Despite the arrival of the information age, the explosion in information resources and services, and the transformation of user needs and behaviors, fewer individuals are choosing librarianship as a profession. This is frequently attributed to low salaries, librarians' inability to articulate their value to institutional stakeholders, and the public perception of the value of librarians. One researcher states that salary is "the key motivator" in attracting people to the field. However, even though salary gains are currently outpacing inflation, the actual earning power is lower than it was in 1970 (Matarazzo 2000).

Library Journal and ARL salary surveys document steady growth in technology positions, overall salary gains across the profession, and other gradual, but positive, trends for women and minorities. Respondents to the *Library Journal* surveys average less than 50 percent of MLIS graduates. A high percentage of those respondents indicate they are working in libraries (Carson 1997; Gregory and McCook 1998; Gregory 1999; Gregory and Wohlmuth 2000; Kyrillidou 2000).

It is suspected that a growing number of MLIS graduates are obtaining employment in other, faster-growing sectors of the information economy instead of libraries. Recent positive news coverage has focused on the high desirability of librarian-type competencies in finding and organizing content, understanding copyright law and licensing issues, and interpreting client needs— all of which are skills especially valued by businesses seeking to build their Web presence (Ainsbury 2000; Quint 2000).

The image of the traditional librarian may be changing for the better as well. The popular press notes that public and college librarians are "needed now more than ever" to help users find what they need on the Internet (*Boston Globe* 2001; *Chicago Sun-Times* 2001; Keller 2000; Wilson 2001; Mallory 2001).

Although enrollment in library schools, information studies programs, or other MLIS-equivalent programs appears to be on the upswing after close to twenty years in decline, the impetus is likely coming from the information-rich growth areas in business services, engineering and management services, and social services—not libraries in the academic sector. It is critical to note that projected job growth for libraries in the education sector, which includes academic libraries, school libraries, and public libraries, is essentially nil for the next decade (Crosby 2000). It is also significant that academic and public libraries account for 62 percent of librarian employment—the same sector where the bulk of the decade's retirements are going to occur.

How Do We Recruit?

The most comprehensive list of employment sources in print remains the Bowker Annual *Guide to Employment Sources in Library and Information Science*, which shows a continuing steady growth in the number of job hotlines and job boards, as well as listservs and other announcement services maintained by associations, school organizations, government agencies, and others. The number of Web sites and listservs with job announcements as a measure of online presence is growing quickly as would be expected (Moore 2000).

A 1997 survey of Internet recruitment methods indicated that all types of libraries are using the Internet successfully in some manner, with academic libraries using it most frequently. The most common method is to post job announcements on electronic mail lists and library Web sites. At the same time, libraries did not, as a rule, solicit electronic resumes or use Internet-based job boards or other online tools as of 1997 (Nesbeitt 1999).

A recent Public Library Association report on recruitment issues and strategies suggested hiring marketing professionals to improve the image of the profession through an aggressive national public relations campaign designed to establish the library as a high-quality employer with a flexible and family-friendly work environment. The PLA report also introduced several more forward-thinking concepts, such as defining career paths within the library at all levels, selecting and training mentors, and creating a "new planning process... to confront stagnant mentalities." The report also highlighted partnerships with MLIS programs and support for MLIS training for in-house staff (PLA 2000).

LIBRARY SCHOOL RECRUITMENT

Although this paper is primarily concerned with professional employment, efforts to attract individuals to MLIS-type degree programs are also critical to the long-term goal. The last formal survey on library school recruitment methods and strategies was published in 1986 (Spivack et al. 1986).

Librarians need to work harder to impart the changing nature of the profession—to call attention to its more "socially active," exciting, challenging aspects in order to attract more high-caliber students to MLIS programs (Bosseau and Martin 1995). Academic librarians tend to come into the profession "by accident," suggesting that information about the profession needs to be aimed at students much earlier, perhaps as early as middle school, using conduits such as Future Information Professionals of America types of organizations.

OUTSIDE LIBRARY-LAND: ONLINE RECRUITING

Looking outside the library literature, online recruiting is the venue of choice for new professionals, especially in Web industries, and business literature is giving it a high priority. The growth of Internet recruiting and employment resources and tools has changed the way employees find jobs and the way employers find hires. The shortness of the hiring cycle is the most visible change. The sheer size of the total applicant pool suggests opportunity for libraries: for instance, almost 18 million employee profiles or resumes are available on monster.com, in addition to an uncounted number on some 5,000 other, smaller job boards. About four million people used the monster.com site to look for work on a "recent" Monday, presumably in the fall of 2000. Of course, there are pitfalls in this area, among them screening mechanisms that could eliminate adverse numbers of minority applicants on non-skill-based criteria. Future enhancements in this industry include more standardized coding for skills and credentials, and more off-the-shelf skills and personality tests (Cappelli 2000).

CHANGING ROLES OF PROFESSIONAL AND PARAPROFESSIONAL STAFF

ARL Newsletter 208/209 summarized many of the key issues surrounding staffing changes in research libraries gleaned from analysis of years of salary and other survey data. The number of redesigned positions and institutional reorganizations in recent years is direct evidence that the profession is in the midst of "watershed change." Non-MLIS "functional specialists" are increasingly employed in business services, personnel, systems, and other administrative areas. Shifts in hiring priorities to meet needs for new skill sets and competencies are resulting in movement from "traditional" library preparation and MLIS education in general (Wilder 2000).

Descriptions in the *Occupational Outlook Handbook* and recent paraprofessional and professional vacancies listed on various national and regional listservs show a significant degree of overlap in public service tasks between professional and paraprofessional (BLS 2000). It can be deduced from ARL survey data that libraries continue to value the MLIS credential but increasingly hire noncredentialed employees and assign them tasks formerly the exclusive province of librarians. The use of the "MLIS or equivalent education or experience" language typical in many professional job requirements is the most visible example (ARL 1995; 2000a, b).

A more significant trend is apparent here. Recent shifts in the staffing of public services positions mirror the movement of paraprofessionals into technical services positions beginning more than a decade ago and highlight the level of service provided by non-MLIS staff in public service areas formerly reserved for professional librarians, such as reference and instruction (Bordeianu and Seiser 2000; Deiss 2000). The successful use of non-MLIS staff in answering reference questions, conducting tours and orientation programs, developing Web pages, and creating instructional materials and leading instruction classes and sessions has been documented as well (Womack and Rupp-Serrano 2000). This is significant given the 46 percent growth in numbers of existing reference positions since 1983, as well as the fact that some 75 percent of job vacancies in 2000 were in public services (Blixrud 2000).

Staffing the reference desk with non-MLIS paraprofessionals is far from new, as is the triage model of paraprofessionals referring complex questions to more experienced librarians. What has changed dramatically over time, however, is the increased competencies and overall skill level of the frontline paraprofessionals, a fact that may have been overlooked by administrators in recent years (Dillon et al. 1998; Deiss 2000). As noted in the PLA report, neglected career paths for paraprofessionals and depressed salaries have served to diminish an individual's likelihood of choosing to work in a library in support capacities, not to mention pursuing a professional credential.

Although the stagnant paraprofessional career path probably exists in most academic libraries at this time, change in this area could be on the forefront. A new job family was recently created at a major university health sciences library to provide new incentives for career growth in ranks spanning paraprofessional through professional. Promotion within the health information analyst career ladder is based on developing expertise outside primary assigned areas, participating in additional projects, and taking on added responsibilities. The highest rank requires completion of a post-MLIS-level internship in library science (Hubber et al. 1999).

CONCLUSION

Opinion on the appropriate mix of professional and support staff will likely range widely as libraries strive to meet developing user needs with new resources and services. The need for new MLIS graduates will likely depend on how closely changes in the MLIS curricula match needed skills and competencies in a specific library environment. However, it is certain that traditional recruiting and retention methods that focus solely on the MLIS credential are not forward thinking.

Using new recruiting mechanisms such as online job search utilities will enlarge the applicant pool by reaching beyond traditional sources of potential employees. Restructuring career paths within libraries could significantly enhance the attractiveness of library employment to a larger number of individuals.

REFERENCES

Ainsbury, B. 2000 "The Revenge of the Library Scientist," *Online* 23 (6): 60–62 (Nov./Dec.).

Association of Research Libraries. 19XX. *ARL Annual Salary Survey.* Washington, D.C.: ARL, available online from http://www.arl.org/stats/salary/index.html.

———. 2000a. *Changing Roles of Library Professionals,* SPEC Kit 256. Washington, D.C.: ARL.

———. 2000b. *The M.L.S. Hiring Requirement,* SPEC Kit 257. Washington, D.C.: ARL.

———. 1995. *Non-Librarian Professionals,* SPEC Kit 212. Washington, D.C.: ARL.

Blixrud, J. 2000. "Back-Room and Front-Line Changes," *ARL* 208/209, 14–15.

Bordeianu, S., and V. Seiser. 1999. "Paraprofessional Catalogers in ARL Libraries." *College and Research Libraries* 60: 532–40.

Bosseau, D. L., and S. K. Martin. 1995. "The Accidental Profession: Seeking the Best and the Brightest," *Journal of Academic Librarianship* 21 (3): 198–99 (May).

Bureau of Labor Statistics. 2000. *Occupational Outlook Handbook,* Washington, D.C.: Bureau of Labor Statistics, Department of Labor, available online from http://www.bls.government/ocohome.htm.

Cappelli, P. 2000. "Making the Most of On-Line Recruiting," *Harvard Business Review* 79 (3): 139–46.

Carson, H. 1997. "Counting on Technology [Placements and Salaries 96]", *Library Journal* 122: 27–33 (Oct. 15).

"College librarians Remain Busy in the Age of the Internet." 2001. *Chicago Sun-Times*, Jan. 9, 7.

Crosby, Olivia. 2000. "Librarians: Information Experts in the Information Age." *Occupational Outlook Quarterly* 44 (4): 1–15 (winter).

Deiss, K. 2000. "Changing Roles in Research Libraries," *ARL* 208/209, 15.

Dillon, J., et al. 1998. "Sharing the Wealth: Paraprofessionals at Oregon State University Valley Library." *OLA Quarterly* 4 (3) (fall), available online from http://www.olaweb.org/quarterly/quar4-3/dillon.shtml.

Gregory, Vicki L. 1999. "Beating Inflation Now," *Library Journal* (Oct. 15): 36–42.

Gregory, Vicki L., and K. de la Pena McCook. 1998. "Breaking the $30K Barrier," *Library Journal* 123: 32–38 (Oct. 15).

Gregory, Vicki L., and S. R. Wohlmuth. 2000. "Better Pay, More Jobs," *Library Journal* 125 (17): 30–36 (Oct. 15).

Huber, J. T., et al. 1999. "Designing an Alternative Career Ladder for Library Assistants," *Bulletin of the Medical Library Association* 87 (1): 74–77 (Jan.).

Keller, L. 2000. "Not an Endangered Career: Looking It Up," CNN.com. Available online from http://www.cnn.com/2000/CAREER/trends/11/28/librarians/.

Kyrillidou, Martha. 2000. "Salary Trends Highlight Inequities—Old and New," *ARL* 208/209: 6–12.

Mallory, M. 2001. "Tech Jobs: Librarians Breaking Out of the Bookish Mold." *The Atlanta Constitution*, Feb. 28, 2001, 15D.

Matarazzo, J. M. 2000. "Who Wants to be a Millionaire (Sic Librarian!)," *Journal of Academic Librarianship*, 26 (5): 309–10.

Moore, M. 2000. "Guide to Employment Sources in the Library and Information Professions," in *2000 Bowker Annual*. New York, Bowker: 297–318.

Nesbeitt, S. L. 1999. "Trends in Internet-Based Library Recruitment: An Introductory Survey." *IRSQ: Internet Reference Services Quarterly* 4 (2), available online from http://webhost.bridgew.edu/snesbeitt/recruit_article.htm.

"Out in the Field: Hiring Demand, Salaries Rise for Librarians." 2001. *Boston Globe*, Jan. 12, M2.

Public Library Association. 2000. "Recruitment of Public Librarians: A Report to the Executive Committee of the Public Library Association." *Public Libraries* 39 (3): 168–72 (May/June), available online from http://www.pla.org/recruitment.html.

Quint, Barbara. 2000. "Recruiting a Corporate Dream Team [librarians make great additions to information industry organizations]," *Information Today* 17 (8): 12–13.

Spivack, J. F., et al. 1986. "A Survey of Recruiting Activities in the Field of Library/Information Science," in *1986 Bowker Annual.* New York, R.R. Bowker, 285–89.

St. Lifer, Evan. 2000. "The Boomer Brain Drain: The Last of Generation?" *Library Journal* 125 (8): 38–42 (May 1).

Wilder, S. 2000. "The Changing Profile of Research Library Professionals," *ARL* 208/209: 1–5 (Feb/Apr).

Wilson, C. 2001. "Stacks of Reasons to Be Thankful for Librarians," *USA Today,* Jan. 17, 1D.

Womack, K., and K. Rupp-Serrano. 2000. "The Librarian's Apprentice: Reference Graduate Assistants." *Reference Services Review* 28: 119–29.

Compiled by Jennifer Sweeney
University of California at Davis
April 2001

Appendix C
Annotated Bibliography

2000 (Dec.). "Undergrad programs the rage [LJ News]." *Library Journal* 125: 22.
Undergrad programs in information studies are reporting enrollment growth; 600 at FSU; 475 at Syracuse. Starting salaries average $41,000, discouraging students who average $10,000 less from pursuing an MLIS . UNC Chapel Hill has started constructing an undergrad program as well.

2001. "Out in the Field: Hiring Demand, Salaries Rise for Librarians." *Boston Globe*, Jan. 12, M2.
Rapid rise in information technology, "record" numbers of librarians retiring are spurring demand for librarians. Approximately 10,000 librarians are retiring annually, double the rate of ten years ago (James Matarazzo, Dean Simmons College School of Library and Information Science). Librarians also being courted for higher-paying private-sector tech jobs such as Webmaster, database manager, information specialist. BLS projects growth in librarian salaries of 11 percent per year in some corporate fields. Public/government library growth predicted at 5 percent. Although 3/4 of jobs in coming years will be in schools, colleges, and public libraries, business services and Internet companies will be the most active recruiters of librarians.

2001. "College librarians remain busy in the age of the Internet." *Chicago Sun-Times,* Jan. 9, 7.

Ainsbury, B. 2000. "The Revenge of the Library Scientist." *Online* 23 (6): 60–62 (Nov./Dec.).
Training in information evaluation and organization. Ability to understand user needs makes librarians excellent additions to Web staff/dot.com businesses, but "librarians don't know it." "20 years since information retrieval world was dominated by MLIS majors." Librarians have not been heavily involved with dot.coms because they did not have technical knowledge to build information retrieval systems (left up to computer scientists); public service tradition in conflict with innovator/entrepreneur, with profit motive; librarians reactive, not creative. MLIS training focuses on working with existing systems, not inventing new ones.

ARL Annual Salary Survey. Washington, D.C.: Association of Research Libraries. Available online from: http://www.arl.org/stats/salary/index.html.

ARL. 1995. *Non-Librarian Professionals,* SPEC Kit 212. Washington, D.C.: Association of Research Libraries. Available online from http://www.arl.org/spec/specialist.html.
Survey of 1995 ARL libraries on extent of non-MLIS hiring into professional positions. Fifty-nine percent consider applicants without the MLIS for positions including systems, administration, archives, special collections, preservation, access services, and collection development, but fewer for cataloging, reference, and acquisitions. "Other" positions include fee-based services, facilities management, business operations, media center services, development. 750+ job searches conducted by this group of libraries during 1992–1994; 110 positions filled with non-MLIS (same position types as above). Combinations of experience and education considered acceptable: master's or Ph.D. in subject area, prior professional experience. Bachelor's was not listed as option in survey, but several libraries mentioned it as sufficient qualification for certain positions. Problems with definitions: libraries that say they do not hire non-MLIS into "professional" positions do, in fact, hire them for positions that other institutions consider "professional." Noted that ARL surveys typically specify that "professionals" are those with the MLIS; salary survey directs respondents to report salaries of anyone they consider "professional," whether or not they hold the MLIS. Noted that there are functions in libraries for which MLIS is not adequate preparation; ALA considers MLIS the terminal degree. New func-

tions and challenges in systems, management, and administration. Core of professionalism not defined. Survey data do not show any changes in recruitment practices or requirements.

ARL. 1999. *Library Support Staff Position Classification Studies*, SPEC Kit 252. Washington, D.C.: Association of Research Libraries. Available online from http://www.arl.org/spec/speclist.html.
Survey of 59 ARL libraries on how support staff classifications are defined, including description, salary, title. Significant that 41 out of 59 libraries had not reviewed classification schemes within the past three years, and almost half had not reviewed within the past six years. Forty-seven percent are unionized. Complexity of work considered the most important factor in distinguishing among positions, followed by independence in decision-making, supervisory responsibilities, and technical abilities. Salary scales reported in most libraries were similar to campus, system, or larger organizational ranges for clerical position classifications. Raise in pay levels is usual outcome of classification studies, half funded by library and half by organization.

ARL. 2000. *Changing Roles of Library Professionals*, SPEC Kit 256. Washington, D.C.: Association of Research Libraries. Available online from http://www.arl.org/spec/speclist.html.
Survey of 55 libraries; analyzed close to 900 position descriptions posted from 1996 to 1999, looking at the types of positions, whether positions were redesigned, whether technology was involved, or whether the position was related to information literacy, administrative support, development, copyright, contracts, licenses, etc. Not surprisingly, new or redesigned positions tend to emphasize technology, especially instructional or educational technology; reference positions emphasize knowledge of electronic resources, information technology specialists require HTML, XML, or other Web or programming skills. Many organizational structures reengineered, and, in fact, some of the new positions were a by-product of organizational redesign. (Difficult to tell exactly what these redesigns are from the descriptions given: How exactly does a "director of computing and telecommunications" differ from the head of systems?) Other redesigned organizations/positions included a coordinator for a "Service Plus" organization and a reconfiguration of services into four educational teams, with positions requiring technology teaching expertise. MLIS still required for many, but not all. Various other degrees deemed desirable, including computer science, educational or instructional technology, business administration, in addition to academic master's degrees in other disciplines. Significant conclusion

is that libraries have a need for new kinds of expertise and are shifting away from "traditional" library skills and library education in general.

ARL. 2000. *The M.L.S. Hiring Requirement,* SPEC Kit 257. Washington, D.C.: Association of Research Libraries. Available online from http://www.arl.org/spec/speclist.html.
Update of 1995 survey of MLIS as criterion for hiring, faculty status, promotion, tenure. 111 libraries responded; 66 percent require MLIS or equivalent, contrasting moderately with 61 percent in 1995. "Equivalency" language a limitation in interpreting survey results, especially given survey question that asks about "strict" MLIS requirement. Half of libraries report faculty status for librarians; 71 percent of libraries with MLIS requirement also have faculty status. One percent require MLIS for promotion. Forty-two percent of libraries award tenure; another 18 percent have equivalent "continuing appointment" or similar status. Of these, about half require MLIS for hire or tenure. Contradiction between policy and practice was noted in this survey versus the ARL annual salary survey, the latter indicating that libraries are hiring more non-MLIS for professional positions than shown in this SPEC survey, although ARL makes a distinction between "librarians" and "other professional positions." (Ambiguity is misleading; professional is defined in some places as MLIS, in others not.) ARL's conclusion is that equivalent types of educational requirements other than strict MLIS may become more prevalent.

Berry III, J. N. 2000. "Educating for Library Jobs [editorial]." *Library Journal* 125 (17): 6 (Oct. 15).
Job market for librarians very strong. Kaliper report on trends in LIS education indicate more programs tailoring curriculum to needs of employers other than libraries despite statistics that show 93 percent of graduates work in libraries. Although schools have made significant steps, students continue to complain about gaps in library education in business side, accountability, human resources, fundraising, public relations, politics. More current development is needed in public information policy, copyright, management of intellectual content, "host of public policy issues directly related to that complicated mix." Libraries on cutting edge of service in the information society. Library schools have neglected needs of "primary and dominant" market—libraries.

Biele, P., and M. M. Adams. 2000. "Other Duties as Assigned: Emerging Trends in the Academic Library Job Market." *College and Research Libraries* 61 (4): 336–47.

Survey of 900 job announcements (posted in 1996, in print) for position type, degree requirements, other requirements; compared results with 1988 Reser/ Schuneman survey. Decrease in number of positions, especially technical services. Growth in electronic services positions. Growth in number of positions requiring computer experience (83 %; up from 10 % in 1974). Previous work experience required in 55 to 65 percent of all positions. ALA MLIS required in 94 percent of public service and tech services jobs versus 76 percent of electronic services positions. Other advanced degrees required for 35 percent of public services jobs, 10 percent tech, and 14 percent electronic; no significant change from 1988. Mean salaries for electronic services positions was $1,700 higher than tech services and $1,831 higher than public services. Positions that preferred experience did not differ significantly in salary. "Less frequent demand for the MLIS could erode the professional status of librarians" (Foote). Important for systems librarians to understand how information flows into the library and how it is used. Suggests training librarians in the field of systems rather than trying to orient programmers into librarianship.

Blixrud, J. 2000. "Back-room and Front-line Changes." *ARL* 208/209: 14–15. Available online from http://www.arl.org/newsltr/208_209/index.html. More ARL salary data analysis: 46 percent rise in reference positions; catalogers fell by 13 percent. No data collected on support staff.

BLS. 2000. *Occupational Outlook Handbook.* Washington, D.C.: Bureau of Labor Statistics, U.S. Department of Labor. Available online from http:// www.bls.government/ocohome.htm.

BLS. 2000. *National Employment and Wage Data.* Washington, D.C.: Bureau of Labor Statistics, U.S. Department of Labor. Available online from http:// www.bls.government/.

Bordeianu, S., and V. Seiser. 1999. "Paraprofessional Catalogers in ARL Libraries." *College and Research Libraries* 60 (6): 532–40. Trend in technical services staffing toward more paraprofessionals and fewer professional librarians observed since 1977; support staff assuming increased levels of responsibility. 1998 survey of ARL libraries showed that majority use paraprofessionals for most copy cataloging, a few for original cataloging. Wide range of education/experience, but on-the-job training highly important all around: "workplace is still the preferred place to learn cataloging." Educational/ experience requirements vary but are generally lower than for professionals (76 % require bachelor's). Although education/experience varies widely among libraries, performance expectations are very similar. LIS schools not providing training for growing need for copy catalogers.

Bosseau, D. L., and S. K. Martin. 1995. "The Accidental Profession: Seeking the Best and the Brightest." *Journal of Academic Librarianship* 21 (3): 198–99 (May).
Acknowledges historically poor recruitment performance of libraries. Common for individuals to discover library profession from other careers. Disappointment at quality, energy of individuals coming out of MLIS programs; not doing enough to attract high-caliber students to profession. Changing nature of the profession: more socially active, exciting, challenging; need to impart this to students at younger ages. Suggests Future Information Professionals of America type of organization aimed at students as far down as middle school, modeled after Future Educators of America. Recommendations of 1991 Strategic Visions Steering Committee (ALA?) including: publicizing "unique advantage" of information age; strengthening LIS programs; developing relationships with other information-related disciplines; establishing alternatives for attaining professional credentials; incorporating different competencies/professionals into info delivery environment; addressing importance of continuing professional education. Lack of participation at college career days and similar forums.

Cappelli, P. 2001. "Making the Most of On-line Recruiting." *Harvard Business Review* 79 (3): 139–46.
Growth of Internet recruiting and employment resources and tools has changed the way employees find jobs and the way employers find hires. "Increasingly well-informed and restless applicant pool and workforce." Hiring cycle shorter. Monster.com database contains more than 18 million employee profiles/resumes; typical recent Monday site logged about 4 million people using it to look for work. Close to 5,000 other, smaller job boards. Employer product information/company information very important in attracting candidates. Electronic screening can include salary, start date, and skill assessments; focus must be on job performance. Caution on screening that may result in adverse/discriminatory rejection profiles. Personality tests okay, tests that identify psychological problems not okay. Growth in skill certifications by outside agencies; one in eight IT jobs already requires some type of certification. Expected: development of standards for describing applicant characteristics; most online recruiting companies already use common definitions for job requirements,

coding applicant experiences.

Carson, H. 1997. "Counting on Technology [Placements and Salaries 96]." *Library Journal* 122 (Oct. 15, 1997): 27–33.
Average salaries grew by 1.7 percent over 1995; half working time spent on technology-related tasks 23 hours/week). 1,924 grads responded out of 4,136 grads total; 27.6 percent said to have taken nontraditional positions, but does not define nontraditional; 89.3 percent said to take permanent full-time; 10 percent permanent part-time. 1995 survey defined "traditional" as a position in an academic, public, school, or special library in acquisitions, cataloging, collection development, media, admin/supervision, adult services, reference, or youth services. According to this definition, systems positions are nontraditional.

Coe, A. 2001. *Overview of Proposed Certified Public Library Administrator (CPLA) Certification Program.* Washington, D.C.: ALA Midwinter. Available online from http://www.pla.org/cpla/index.html.
Proposed post-MLIS certification program for public librarians, focusing on business/finance, fundraising, facilities, organization and personnel management, technology, strategic planning, serving diverse populations, current issues. Presented by ALA Committee on Education to ALA Council at ALA Midwinter, January 2001.

Council on Library and Media Technicians (COLT). 2001.
Association for support staff started in 1967; significant growth in 1990s. Web site contains information on resources, links; online journal contains articles on wide range of library operations, services, humor, fiction, poetry. Available online from: http://library.ucr.edu/COLT/.

Crosby, O. 2001. "Librarians: Information Experts in the Information Age." *Occupational Outlook Quarterly* 44, no.4 (winter 2000-2001): 1–15. Available online from http://www.bls.government/opub/ooq/ooqhome.htm.
Conservative profile of librarianship tasks and skills emphasizes uses of computer applications and resources; essential mission/function unchanged. Employment outlook: number of jobs in all types of libraries expected to grow 5 percent, on average, between 1998 and 2008; zero growth expected in education (academic, school, public libraries). Highest growth expected in industries outside education: business services (87 % growth expected), museums and zoos (51 %), social services (44 %), engineering/management services (39 %). Effect of technology: increased complexity of reference questions, expanded librar-

ians' teaching roles, expanded job prospects to fields outside education as well as outside libraries. Demand for technical skills translating into higher salaries.

Deiss, K. 2000. "Changing Roles in Research Libraries." *ARL* 208/209: 15. Available online from http://www.arl.org/newsltr/208_209/index.html. Rise in redesigned positions, especially in technology-related positions, user services, collection development.

Dillon, J., et al. 1998. "Sharing the Wealth: Paraprofessionals at Oregon State University Valley Library." *OLA Quarterly* (4): 3 (fall). Description of shift from triage model to full integration of paraprofessionals on an academic library reference desk. Conclusion is that professionals and paraprofessional both have skills and experience contributing to successful reference performance. In most cases, "service quality is based more on a friendly, eager-to-be-of-service attitude than on educational background."

Greenhouse, S. 2000. "Proposed Raise for Librarians Dropped after City Objects." *New York Times,* Sep. 17, 46. NYPL withdrew proposal to raise librarian salaries 15 percent after city objected on grounds the proposal did not include increase in workweek to 37.5 hrs. Starting salary is $31k, median $39k. Branches nearing a staffing crisis, most do not have children's librarians. City also objected to proposed cuts in services and book budget.

Gregory, V. L., and K. d. l. P. McCook. 1998. "Breaking the $30K Barrier." *Library Journal* 123 (17): 32–38 (Oct. 15). Average beginning salary $30, 270, a 2.7 percent increase up from 1.7 percent in 1996. CPI increase was 1.5 percent; median salary increased 5.4 percent. Significant gains in minority salary—up 6.12 percent. Placements in libraries account for 93 percent; 83 percent are permanent full-time. Technology jobs— systems, Webmaster, telecommunications—reported salaries 12 percent higher than average. 2,151 graduates responded to survey out of 4,370. Moderate increase in number of placements reported in special libraries. Students mentioned emphasis on technology in interviewing; many cited lack of training on cutting-edge technology skills.

Gregory, V. L. 1999. "Beating Inflation Now." *Library Journal* 124 (17): 36–42 (Oct. 15). Salaries jump 5.4 percent, outpacing inflation; increases in numbers of openings.

Gregory, V. L., and S. R. Wohlmuth. 2000. "Better Pay, More Jobs." *Library Journal* 125 (17): 30–36 (Oct. 15).
Average beginning salary up 6.5 percent from 1998; last year's gain 5.4 percent, outpacing CPI two years in a row. Placement in types of jobs consistent; 83.5 percent in permanent professional library positions. Reported number of positions listed at schools was up slightly at about one-third of the schools. College/university library placements up significantly from previous year. Grads say they need more instruction in traditional areas—reference, online searching, cataloging, collection development, in addition to technical; accounting/ business management also mentioned. Nontraditional job offerings seem to offer more pay, benefits, professional development, etc., than traditional library positions. 4,201 grads total; 1,765 responded to survey. (Comments: large number of unreporting graduates with unknown status (59 %); students' stated desire for more traditional courses contradicts complaints from employers that students are exiting LIS programs without core competencies.)

Huber, J. T., et al. 1999. "Designing an Alternative Career Ladder for Library Assistants." *Bulletin of the Medical Library Association* 87(1): 74–77 (Jan.).
New career path for library assistants developed using incentive system to recognize enhanced skill sets. Promotion based on developing expertise outside primary area, participation in additional projects, and taking on added responsibilities. Highest rank in new job family (health information analyst) requires completion of post-master's library science internship.

Staff interview March 2001. Staff/librarian divide.
Staff versus librarian divide not just attitude problem not referring to positions filled by students. Staff not able to advance in rank based on skill development or length of service; staff positions not viewed as career-type appointments even though many individuals hold jobs for 10+ years. Staff positions classed by task type, not by individual's skill level (e.g., LAII will remain so despite growth in abilities and experience). Difficulties when filling positions vacated by someone with greater length of service. Many staff performing tasks formerly done only by librarians, especially in technical services (cataloging, acquisitions); now trend has spread to reference desk service (25 % of hours at specialized reference desks filled by staff). Frustrations felt by staff include perceived inequities in compensation, lack of ability to advance in rank, feelings of mistrust/anger stemming from librarians' attitudes that certain tasks should

not be performed by staff because they lack the MLIS. Lack of recognition of value of staff also reflected in interview process: 20-minute brief questioning for LAs versus lengthy librarian recruitment process.

Joinson, C. 2001. "Refocusing Job Descriptions." *HR Magazine* 46 (1): 66–72. "And other duties as assigned" a trap for HR managers dealing with rapidly changing work environments/requirements. Difficulties with traditional job descriptions that attempt to narrowly match specific skills and tasks, especially when skills no longer match actual work activities. Some managers now basing job descriptions on the role the position plays in the work environment, describing broader abilities/competencies associated with job roles, also using performance goals—all of which allow more flexibility to meet varying demands as technology/customer needs change. Job descriptions also helpful for both employee and employer in defining career and growth goals. Using successful behavior of top performers to define job roles, expectations of managers. Example: Computer programmer success will depend on ability to upgrade skills; competency would include self-directed learning. Strong performance management system is also needed; best if measured against goals rather than specific tasks. Performance plans as "living job descriptions" are also strong defense against employment claims involving discrimination, ADA, negligence, retaliation, etc. Cautions: Unions may favor job descriptions, which tend to limit responsibilities; managers need to keep union informed of changes in job description structure. Also higher risk of contract violation grievances if out-of-date job descriptions are neglected and supervisors or others appear to be doing work that belongs to bargaining unit members.

Keller, L. 2000. "Not an Endangered Career: Looking It Up." CNN.com. Public librarian notes that librarians are needed more than ever to help people find what they are looking for given the enormous amount of information available to everybody on the Internet. "Information glut daunting and confusing." Market Data Retrieval research shows 2,634 reference librarians employed in public libraries in 1995; today, 4,100. Internet is not driving people away from libraries, just the opposite. Print medium will not be totally replaced by electronic; it will be augmented.

Kyrillidou, M. 2000. "Salary Trends Highlight Inequities—Old and New." *ARL* 208/209, 6–12. Available online from http://www.arl.org/newsltr/208_209/index.html. Analysis of ARL annual salary survey. Although purchasing power has stayed ahead of inflation, higher salaries are rising faster than lower salaries. Geographical analysis of differentials across U.S.: highest salaries in Pacific region, New England, and Middle Atlantic; these regions also have the slowest increases; mountain region salaries increasing the fastest. Library type: Large private universities continue to pay the most as they have since 1988 when they outpaced public institutions. Large state university libraries pay the least, although increases have been higher than average. Sex: In this predominantly female profession, salary differential is small, with women earning 99 percent of men's salaries, up from 86 percent in 1980. No experience difference. Women continue to be underrepresented and underpaid in comparison to men in top management positions. Functional specialist positions have more men and also pay men higher salaries; opposite of reference librarian positions, which have more women, yet also pay men more. Poses question of whether increased technical sophistication of functional specialists as compared to service orientation of reference positions has effect on salary; sex-stereotyping? Racial/ethnic groups underrepresented in ARL libraries compared to other academic libraries; certain groups predominant in specific geographic areas (African American in south, Asian in NE and Pacific), salary levels coincide.

Kyrillidou, M. 2000. "Educational Credentials, Professionalism, and Librarians." *ARL* 208/209, 12–13. Available online from http://www.arl.org/newsltr/ 208_209/index.html.
ARL varies in its definitions of librarian and professional, adding to the ambiguity of the library community when it comes to defining roles. The salary survey takes a broader view, including as "professionals" positions in systems, personnel, budget, etc., who are not MLIS librarians. Some SPEC surveys, on the other hand, use narrow construction of professional MLIS. Statistics on perceived policy and actual hiring vis-à-vis the MLIS requirement have reversed themselves at least once according to a brief overview of the past decade: in the early-mid 1990s, 59 percent of libraries reported that they were willing to consider non-MLIS applicants and 64 percent reported actually hiring non-MLIS, in a total of 110 hires. A more recent SPEC survey showed that fewer libraries are willing to consider non-MLIS, but the salary survey indicates that more are, in fact, being hired. Since 1985, the numbers of non-MLIS professionals have at least doubled. Conclusion is that the term "professional" in libraries does not have a consistent meaning, and more study is needed from entities such at the ALA Congress on Professional Education. Analysis is confounded by small sample size, inconsistent terminology.

Lippincott, J. 2000. "Librarians and Cross-sector Teamwork." *ARL* 208/209, 22–23. Available online from http://www.arl.org/newsltr/208_209/index.html. Increased need for collaboration/cooperation between libraries and institutions they support. Individuals recruited for new positions, especially in technology areas, Web/electronic services, need to have team orientation, understand roles of players outside library. No one group has expertise in all areas to accomplish programmatic, policy goals. Libraries not yet involved in true partnerships involving common mission, mutual benefit. Librarian as guest lecturer providing BI rather than collaborating with faculty to develop integrated curriculum. Past limitations: Focusing on parochial interests; criticizing motives, work style of team members, not being open to broader points of view. Librarian's fear of losing identity. Increasing importance of social skills, willingness to appreciate and understand perspective of those outside the library. Managers need to help staff think in broader terms, reward collaboration.

Mallory, M. 2001. "Tech Jobs: Librarians breaking out of the Bookish Mold." *Atlanta Constitution*, Feb. 28, 15D.
Internet plays central role in how librarians do their work, which includes designing Web pages, creating online publications as part of helping people find information. "MLIS is the minimum educational requirement."

Matarazzo, J. M. 2000. "Who Wants to Be a Millionaire (Sic Librarian!)?" *Journal of Academic Librarianship* 26 (5): 309–10.
Salary is key motivator to attracting people to the library profession; as long as salaries are low, students will not pursue the qualification. Historical data back to the 1950s show that librarian shortages and low salaries go hand in hand. Value of starting salaries in 1970 were actually higher than those ten years later in current dollars; MLIS grad rates also declined 40 percent from 1974 to 1985. Although salaries have kept pace with (and even outpaced in recent years) inflation, there still has been no gain in actual earning power in 30 years. Echoes economic status of other education professions, which have charted net losses in earning power. "Single most important source of recruitment" is referral by professionals in the field. Although high job satisfaction continues to be a motivator for entry into the field, it is not enough to draw in the best and the brightest.

Moore, M. 2000. *Guide to Employment Sources in the Library and Information Professions,* in *Bowker Annual.* New York: R.R. Bowker, 297–318.
Sources focus on professional positions, including print library literature,

Internet, telephone job lines, specialized library associations/groups, state library agencies and associations, MLIS programs, federal employment sources, others. A few carry information on support staff/paraprofessionals; noted that these positions are more often recruited through local sources.

Nesbeitt, S. L. 1999. "Trends in Internet-based Library Recruitment: An Introductory Survey." *IRSQ: Internet Reference Services Quarterly* 4 (2). Available online from http://webhost.bridgew.edu/snesbeitt/recruit_article.htm.
1997 survey of 70 academic, public, and special libraries documents use of Internet for recruiting and job searching. Type of use, perceived success of posting, actual responses received of print sources. Internet for recruiting used mostly by academic libraries; types of positions are same as those in print sources. Mailing lists with national scope were the most productive online recruitment tool. Most employers do not search or use online resume banks; about half of the academic libraries accept electronic resumes. Most employers do not plan to scale down print advertising.

Pettigrew, K. E., and J. C. Durrance. 2000. *KALIPER Study Identifies Trends in Library and Information Science Education.* New York: R.R. Bowker, 208–18.
Kellogg-ALISE Information Professions and Education Reform Project (KALIPER) examined nature and extent of major changes in LIS curriculum in U.S., Canada, and England. Project included surveys of 26 LIS schools, interviews with deans/directors, case studies, and analyses of curricula, job announcements, and faculty specialty descriptors. Study identified six trends: (1) LIS curriculum addressing broader base of information environments and problems; (2) core curriculum continues to incorporate multidisciplinary perspectives and is predominantly user centered; (3) LIS schools are increasing investment and infusion of information technology; (4) more flexibility in tailoring programs around specific areas of interest, although not reported or executed with any consistency; a variety of approaches springing up, from electives to modifying core requirements; (5) instruction being offered in different formats for more flexibility, especially in length, and location (distance education significant growth area; interuniversity partnerships); and (6) LIS expanding programs by offering related degrees/certificates at master's, bachelor's, and doctoral levels. Wide range of areas include business, computer science, electrical engineering, English, history, theatre/television, law. Current changes have been prompted by student/employer demands; professional association demands for grad competencies; growth of emerging technology; internal campus relationships; competition from other programs; availability of financial support from

innovation. Concerns for future include shortage of LIS Ph.D.s; need to build and promote LIS core knowledge despite rush of other disciplines "into LIS." What is relationship between information and technology? Is LIS a profession or a discipline?

PLA. 2000. "Recruitment of Public Librarians: A Report to the Executive Committee of the Public Library Association." *Public Libraries* 39 (3): 168–72. Available online from http://www.pla.org/recruitment.html.
PLA committee surveyed libraries on recruitment tactics: newspaper ads, library press, LIS announcements, Internet. Most effective: Internet, local ads, in-house incentives. Recommendations for boosting MLIS enrollment as well as public library employment. Recommendations include hiring professional marketing consultant for PR campaign; recruiting LIS students from nontraditional workers; forming partnerships with LIS programs to recruit new librarians; identifing distance learning MLIS programs; selecting and training mentors; creating new "planning process... confront stagnant mentalities and challenge assumptions." Define career paths within library at all levels; establish library as high-quality employer; emphasize flexible hours/work schedules. Hire benefits consultant to benchmark library benefits with other information professions. Explore undergraduate LIS degree. Other issues: Inadequate understanding of library profession; inflexible organizations; lack of encouragement in LIS toward public libraries; lack of minorities; no "umbrella recruitment plan".

Quint, B. 2000. "Recruiting a Corporate Dream Team [librarians make great additions to information industry organizations]." *Information Today* 17 (8): 12–13.
Extolling the value of librarians as extremely knowledgeable about finding and organizing content, intelligent regarding copyright laws, licensing, high standards, hard working, ethical. Couple of digs at traditional stereotypes/misinformation about "obsessive types" who are into Library of Congress, MARC-record, AACRII, "you don't need to hire them....Most library schools these days tell students about the formal systems, but they don't often train them." Need to nurture and heighten librarians' sense of self-worth, low self-esteem noted. Need to pay them well in order to keep the library schools open.

Ray, M. 2000. "Making Systems Visible." *ARL* 208/209, 24.
Using systems approach to develop small-scale, high-impact change; find leverage. Shift in pay scale/job titles at University of Arizona, both support staff

and professional: support staff titles were paid in lowest quartile, lots of overlap on pay scale, new hires paid as much as/more than existing experienced employees. New scale involved redistributing titles out of library assistant/library supervisor into library specialists, raising pay. Overall organization shows more professionals, fewer support staff than a decade ago; twice as many specialists, and half as many supervisors.

Schneider, K. G. 2000. "My Money, My Life; The Librarian's Image, Unrevised." *New York Times* Oct. 29, 11.
Although large parts of the country are unable to attract and keep employees for the public libraries because of low pay and lack of health care benefits, personal core values of the helping professions such as librarians, educators, child care, ministry can be more important than money.

Spivack, J. F., et al. 1986. "A Survey of Recruiting Activities in the Field of Library/Information Science," in *1986 Bowker Annual.* New York: R.R. Bowker, 285–89.
NCLIS/ALISE survey of 46 LIS schools on recruitment methods. All use various mixes of advertising, publications, direct mail, and personal contacts; alumni referral appears the most effective. Most budgets around $1,000–$2,000. No online methods. Lack of recruitment by associations and lack of innovation/creativity in marketing materials noted.

St. Lifer, E. 2000. "The Boomer Brain Drain: The Last of Generation?" *Library Journal* 125(8): 38–42 (May 1).
Increasing retirements heightening demand while low pay stifles supply. Typical for librarians with master's degrees to earn less than individuals with undergraduate degrees; allure of public service in the 1960s and 1970s was stronger than today. Informal poll at PLA conference showed 26 job seekers for 230 openings. Trend is recent: ALA conference 1997 had 1,105 job seekers for 472 jobs; 1998 had 545 seekers for 874 jobs; 1999 had 489 seekers for 997 jobs. Average starting salary $31,915. Dearth of librarians is especially bad for smaller libraries far from major cities. Unconfirmed variable is number of library school grads who are choosing jobs outside libraries. *LJ* survey on aging showed that 44 percent of current librarians said if they were a recent graduate, they would not pursue a career in librarianship given the "wealth" of opportunities today. Opinion varies; library schools report enrollment starting to surge again. Some schools are partnering with libraries to prepare paraprofessionals for MLIS. "We need to spend more time thinking about how we would staff libraries with

the people we can hire rather than spending so much time fretting over the people we can't." Also need to look at what skills are really needed, including how to become teaching organizations. Libraries' lack of articulation on professional responsibilities. No clear picture of what work requires MLIS and what does not. Media misinformation regarding low growth potential, image. Need to retool expertise as information mediators solidify and expand role in institutions; engage communities in different ways.

U.S. Dept. of Education, N. C. E. S. 2000. "Integrated Postsecondary Education Data System (IPEDS), Higher Education General Information Survey (HEGIS), and 'Completions' surveys, Digest of Education Statistics, Financial Statistics of Institutions of Higher Education (various tables)." Available online from http://nces.ed.government/ipeds/index.html; http://nces.ed.government/pubs2001/digest/.

2001. "What is information studies ? Undergraduates." Florida State University School of Information Studies. Available online from http://www.lis.fsu.edu/Prospects/WhatIS.cfm.
Web site describes field of information studies without mentioning libraries. Focus is on interaction of user with information products, services, and organizations. Goal of program is to "provide the knowledge, skills, and values required to develop, organize, store, retrieve, administer, and facilitate the use of recordable information and knowledge." No mention of degree offered (listed in ALA directory as offering master's and doctoral).

White, H. 1998. "White Papers: What Is a Professional in Our Field? [editorial]." *Library Journal* 123 (3): 117–18 (Feb. 15).
Organizations require mix of skills, including clerical (terminology aside) and professional librarian. Library context confusing because of visibility of clerical duties and tendency of nonprofessional staff to take on professional duties (answering reference questions, for example). Unfair to users to allow this; presents misleading image of library work. Compares library professionals doing clerical work and vice versa to doctors mopping floors or nurse's aides doing surgery. Difference is users cannot tell the difference between professional and nonprofessional in libraries. Suggests using the definition of professional used in Fair Labor Standards Act 1910, exempt versus nonexempt. Requiring MLIS credential will help ensure need for professional status of librarians. What about communities that cannot afford "librarians" and hire clerks, instead. Staffing mix has been changed by technology; jobs of professional librarians even

more important—"those who do what machines cannot." LIS perpetuating "self-trivialization" by training for less expensive technological certification rather than master's-level professional degree. Unwillingness of state legislatures to fund libraries at appropriate levels. As professionals we should not "do more with less"; gives up professional identity. Professions "compete... for emerging problems and strive to expand jurisdiction by ... pre-empting the activities of other professions" (Andrew Abbott, *The System of Professions*).

Wilder, S. 2000. "The Changing Profile of Research Library Professionals." *ARL* 208/209: 1–5 (Feb./Apr.). Available online from http://www.arl.org/ newsltr/208_209/index.html.
Study of historical ARL annual salary survey data. Profession in midst of "watershed change"; libraries shifting hiring priorities to meet needs for new expertise, moving away from traditional library skills/education generally. High retirement levels and overall aging librarian population, especially academic librarians, due to several factors, including overall demographics of baby boom, decline in rate of hire of new professionals, and higher age of MLIS students. Other shifts include doubling in percent of functional specialists hired from 1990 to 1998, and halving of the number of catalogers (other position types such as reference, subject specialist, department head remained steady); overall hiring rate down 25 percent from 1990–1998. Noted that 55 percent of hires in functional specialist categories are not MLIS librarians; areas include systems, archives, personnel. Although average experience is 4.7 years, in contrast to 7.1 years for other categories, average salary is very close to other categories. 91 percent of library directors are over age 60, up from 63 percent in 1990; also older directors are more likely to be male.

Wilson, C. 2001. "Stacks of Reasons to Be Thankful for Librarians." *USA Today*, Jan. 17, 1D.
Librarians still needed to help users find information on the Internet.

Wisner, W. H. 2001. "Librarianship Enters the Twilight [opinion]." *Library Journal* 125 (Jan. 17): 68.
Provocative rant of the traditionalist mourning the death of the library: librarianship is dying, exhibiting the "last rosy glow" before expiring like a tuberculosis victim. Historic mission of libraries is finished, privatization of the book and perfection of technology, e-books will cause libraries to disappear gradually. Interactive media are taking over public's attention, replacing public's interest in books/knowledge, will "subvert culture" from narrative structures to

video images. Librarians have devalued, lost reverence for the word. Incoming professionals want to move away from librarian stereotypes, use different names- information technology, etc. Library schools have not known what to call them- selves either. Equates "selling ourselves" in the marketing sense to prostitution. Librarian's "pursuit of efficiency and convenience" is leading us to perdition at the "vendor's helpful little hands"; "librarians are not drivers on the information superhighway, merely rosy-cheeked hitchikers thumbing a ride."

Womack, K., and K. Rupp-Serrano. 2000. "The Librarian's Apprentice: Refer- ence Graduate Assistants." *Reference Services Review* 28 (2): 119–29.
Survey of 36 academic libraries that employ graduate students in various para- professional positions. Limited to institutions with library science graduate programs. Recruitment strategies: Most hired from LIS programs; other aca- demic disciplines also sources; word of mouth, listserv announcements, class announcements, bulletin boards, "other," including LIS events, referrals from LIS faculty teaching reference courses, campus grad office, counselors. About half are hourly appointees; very low pay (minimum wage to $11.50/hour 1998?, average $6.50); one third salaried. Appointment length varies, most appear to be 15–20 hours/week; work schedules tend toward afternoons/evenings and weekends. One third or fewer offer tuition remission, health insurance. Aver- age length of employment: Half until graduation; half one year. Selection tools: Experience, interview, resume, letter, completion of reference course, faculty recommendation. Duties include reference desk/email reference, library orien- tation/tours, creating instructional materials, conducting BI sessions.

Compiled by Jennifer Sweeney
University of California at Davis
April, 2001

DATE DUE

DATE DUE			
JAN 0 9 2000			
JUL 2 5 2005			
AUG 2 4 2000			
MAR 2 8 2005			
			Printed in USA